T0339872

William Gregg's Civil War

New Perspectives on the Civil War Era

William Gregg's Civil War

The Battle to Shape the History of Guerrilla Warfare

By William H. Gregg

Edited and Annotated by Joseph M. Beilein Jr.

The University of Georgia Press

ATHENS

© 2019 by the University of Georgia Press
Athens, Georgia 30602
www.ugapress.org
All rights reserved
Set in 10/13 ITC New Bskerville Std
by Kaelin Chappell Broaddus

Most University of Georgia Press titles are
available from popular e-book vendors.

Printed digitally

Library of Congress Cataloging-in-Publication Data

Names: Gregg, William H., 1838–1916, author. | Beilein, Joseph M., Jr., editor, author.
Title: William Gregg's Civil War : the battle to shape the history of guerrilla warfare
/ by William H. Gregg ; edited and annotated by Joseph M. Beilein Jr.
Description: Athens, Georgia : University of Georgia Press, [2019] | Series: New
perspectives on the Civil War era | Includes bibliographical references and index.
Identifiers: LCCN 2019007397| ISBN 9780820355795 (hardback : alk. paper) | ISBN
9780820355771 (pbk. : alk. paper) | ISBN 9780820355788 (e-book)
Subjects: LCSH: Gregg, William H., 1838–1916 | Missouri—History—Civil War, 1861–1865—
Underground movements. | Quantrill, William Clarke, 1837–1865—Friends and associates.
| Guerrillas—Confederate States of America—Biography. | Guerrilla warfare—United
States—History—19th century. | Guerrillas—United States—History—19th century.
| United States—History—Civil War, 1861–1865—Underground movements.
Classification: LCC E470.45 .G74 2019 | DDC 973.7/42092 [B] —dc23
LC record available at https://lccn.loc.gov/2019007397

In memory of Bill Rule,
my grandfather, friend, and favorite storyteller.

Contents

List of Illustrations   ix

Acknowledgments   xi

━━━━━

Introduction. The Irregular Creation of Guerrilla History   1

Editorial Method   43

A Little Dab of History
without Embellishment   45

ADDENDA

1. My War Horse Scroggins   80

2. Anderson the Horse Thief   83

3. Gregg Family History   85

4. Documentation of Ownership   88

William H. Gregg–William E. Connelley
Correspondence (1903–1909)   91

━━━━━

Bibliography   113

Index   119

Illustrations

William H. Gregg   3

William E. Connelley   5

Counties of Missouri   11

Map of the Union-occupied district where Gregg primarily fought   13

Map of Baxter Springs   16

William C. Quantrill   28

Acknowledgments

THERE WERE A FEW DEBTS INCURRED while bringing this volume into fruition. Within the profession several colleagues have played significant roles in the publication of the Gregg memoir. First and foremost, I must thank LeeAnn Whites, who either suggested that I try to publish the Gregg memoir or reaffirmed my idea to do so. I honestly can't remember. In either case, she served as a source of inspiration. Matthew Hulbert, a great guerrilla scholar, has been supportive of this project from the moment he heard about it. Judkin Browning's interest in publishing this volume for his series at the University of Georgia Press became the catalyst for turning an idea into a reality. Mick Gusinde-Duffy did a skillful job in getting this manuscript through the process and ultimately to press. Additionally, the reviewers offered important feedback and criticism that helped to shape the final version of this book.

Many personal debts are owed as well. The structure of this project was conceived, and much of the introduction of this work was written, within the walls of the Freeman House at the Miller family's farm at Spring Creek in the summer of 2015. Built in 1876, the Freeman House serves as the perfect place to commune with nature and the ghosts of the past; it provided me with the best possible setting for understanding a man from a different time. Without the generosity of the Miller family, especially Jeff Miller, this book would never have been produced. My own family is also to be thanked: Mom, Dad, Jill, Nick, Joe, Addie, Jane, and Clark. They are always incredibly supportive, even when they are not completely sure what they are supporting. That kind of unconditional support is necessary for a person who is immersed in the strange world of historical study. This book is also a great credit to Rachel, who has patiently listened to me talk about this project, sat next to me in a number of coffee shops while I worked, and helped me to see the big picture when my focus was painfully narrow. Many thanks.

William Gregg's Civil War

Introduction

The Irregular Creation of Guerrilla History

FROM THE OPENING PAGES OF HIS MEMOIR, William H. Gregg, who had fought as a Southern guerrilla in Missouri during the Civil War, was clear about his intentions. "Quantrill and his men," Gregg wrote in the introduction, "have been unjustly slandered by the people of the North, a people who, even to this day, know nothing of them, except what they have read in irresponsible books and newspapers. The time has come when their minds should be disabused." When Gregg wrote these words in the early years of the twentieth century, other Southern men who fought in the war, leaders of the Confederacy such as Robert E. Lee and Thomas "Stonewall" Jackson, as well as common soldiers of the formal Confederate armies, had gained some sympathy from their old enemies. Unlike the heroes of the Lost Cause and the men in gray who reunited with their old enemies on the basis of a shared sacrifice, however, the bushwhackers were still held in contempt by their old foes and even by some of their Southern brethren who thought them merely outlaws and opportunists. Gregg's goal was to demonstrate to the men and women who might read his memoir that the guerrillas deserved to be seen in the same honorable light as the other fighting men.[1]

Gregg's memoir tells the remarkable story of the Civil War as it was experienced by a slaveholding Southern guerrilla from Missouri. Gregg titled the memoir *A Little Dab of History without Embellishment,* emphasizing his commitment to objectivity, but it has been known by historians as the "Gregg manuscript" nearly since its completion in 1906. Regardless of what it has been called, few recollections come close in subject matter, and fewer still present the guerrilla war in Missouri so accurately. Quite simply, the memoir offers an irreplaceable perspective on the war. Fragments of Gregg's history of the war appear in scholarly texts, often out of context and rarely in keeping with the memoir's intended message. Out-

---

1. William H. Gregg, "A Little Dab of History without Embellishment," 1906, State Historical Society of Missouri, Columbia, Mo.

side a handful of professional and amateur historians, however, few people have read the memoir or know of its existence. The Gregg memoir still has significant contributions to make to our historical understanding of the guerrilla war and the Civil War more broadly.[2]

There are omissions, however. Gregg did not write of slavery as a cause of the war or much at all. Like many of his guerrilla comrades, Gregg came from a slaveholding family. Yet when he looked back and remembered the war—the seminal moment of his adult life—he was unable or unwilling to see and comprehend the significance of slavery in its coming. Instead, Gregg filled the void of causation with Union atrocities. Similarly, he refrained from sharing too many of the gory details of guerrilla warfare in Missouri with his readers. In his colorful descriptions of combat, Gregg did not mention the collateral damage felt by Union women and other noncombatants, nor did he write about scalps or mutilation more generally. When one reads the memoir, it is important to keep these omissions in mind: both the conspicuous absence of slavery as a cause and the absence of the intimate violence of guerrilla warfare worked to shape and frame the narrative in powerful ways.[3]

Despite these omissions, Gregg's hopes for publication of his memoir are now realized. Historians, Civil War enthusiasts, and students have the chance to see the war from Gregg's perspective. The memoir is published here in full along with other associated documents that further enrich the already substantial offerings of Gregg's recollection. In particular, this volume includes the surviving correspondence between Gregg and early historian of the guerrilla conflict William E. Connelley. While these letters share interesting tidbits about the war, more importantly, they provide a behind-the-scenes look at how history is made. Gregg's history presents an alternative perspective on the guerrilla war in Missouri—not only a different perspective from the one bandied about by northerners

---

2. The Gregg memoir has been cited in nearly every major historical work on the guerrilla war in Missouri. See Connelley, *Quantrill and the Border Wars*, 222; Brownlee, *Gray Ghosts of the Confederacy*, 55; Castel, *William Clarke Quantrill*, 246; Fellman, *Inside War*, 253–56; Sutherland, *A Savage Conflict*, 363.

3. An important contribution made by scholars of memory has been not only the observation that many of the memoirs written during the turn of the century were silent on the issues of slavery and race but that memoirists had political interests in whitewashing their narratives. Gregg's memoir is representative of this larger trend. For the pathbreaking work on the subject, see Blight, *Race and Reunion*.

William H. Gregg.
From William E. Connelley,
Quantrill and the Border Wars, 341.

in the early twentieth century but also one that challenges some modern interpretations of guerrilla warfare as it was waged in the Civil War.[4] The violence that took place during Gregg's war had great effect on shaping his world, but that violence came and went. Words like those used by Gregg and the other men who survived the war and words that were written later by historians live on, shaping and reshaping the past for generations, long after the ink has dried. In this way, the war still rages. More than any other event in American history, the Civil War is fought and refought through the written word and in American minds.

---

4. The letters can be found in William Elsey Connelley Papers, Denver Public Library; William C. Quantrill Collection, McCain Library and Archives, University of Southern Mississippi, Hattiesburg (hereafter Quantrill Collection); State Historical Society of Missouri, Columbia, Mo.

The story of the Gregg memoir, then, is the story of men and women fighting over the past to win a war for the present. This rare glimpse into the ways that a history, especially a controversial history, is manipulated to fit the circumstances of the present shows us what is lost when stories are cropped to fit a preconceived form.[5]

Students who seek to delve deeper into the ways history is constructed should access the component website that allows students and scholars to interact with the volume's content and sources. Search for this book on www.ugapress.org for links to the bonus material.

William E. Connelley and the Origins of the Gregg Memoir

In the early 1900s, when Gregg sat down to write the story of his experience fighting in the Civil War, thousands of the war's participants and witnesses gave interviews, spoke to audiences, and wrote books about the war as they saw it. For these men and women, the war was the highlight (or the lowlight) of their not-quite-finished time on earth, and they wanted to share their recollections before passing on. In this sense, Gregg was not unique. He was getting older, his body growing more fragile each day, and he feared his story would die with him. As a guerrilla and the right-hand man to William Clarke Quantrill, America's most infamous bushwhacker, Gregg offered the ultimate insider's point of view into the most mysterious group of fighters in the most destructive war on American soil. In other words, his voice was not only essential in the melody that was shaping America's understanding of the Civil War for successive generations, but it also stood out from the growing chorus singing the same old tune about Grant and Lee, the Blue and the Gray, Vicksburg and Gettysburg. All he had to do was get his memoir published.[6]

---

5. For more regarding the construction of guerrilla history, see Beilein and Hulbert, *The Civil War Guerrilla*. For more about the significance of the Civil War today, see McPherson, *The War That Forged a Nation*.

6. There is a growing body of literature regarding memorialization during this period and the dominant narratives that came through. David Blight demonstrates that reconciliation was a significant part of this phenomenon, though others have more recently illustrated that reunification had its limits. See Blight, *Race and Reunion*; Neely, *The Border between Them*; Whites, *Gender Matters*, 95–112. Also see Janney, *Remembering the Civil War*.

William E. Connelley.
Frontispiece from Connelley,
*A Standard History of Kansas
and Kansans*, vol. 1.

Enter William E. Connelley, not a veteran of the war but rather an established amateur historian living in Kansas, just across the state border
from Gregg. In his early works, Connelley studied Kansans such as the
various Native American tribes that inhabited the state before the arrival
of white settlers and the abolitionists who migrated to the embattled territory in the 1850s. At the dawn of the twentieth century, Connelley was
looking beyond the borders of the Sunflower State. He sought to write
the definitive history of Quantrill's guerrillas, who operated mostly along
the Kansas-Missouri border. Connelley wanted to correct the many historical errors created by John N. Edwards, an ex–Confederate cavalryman
and unreconstructed rebel. Edwards's book, *Noted Guerrillas*, published in
1877, presented the guerrillas and especially Quantrill in a glowing light.
The favorable narrative was the product of Edwards's proslavery and pro-
Southern politics and the fact that his book was based on first-person accounts of the guerrillas themselves, men who also happened to be his
friends. To challenge the narrative presented in *Noted Guerrillas*, Connelley
began researching the subject in ways that looked similar to professional
historical methods, though he was not working in the spirit of academic

scholarship. He looked at local documents created before and during the war, dug into military records, and talked to many of the bushwhackers' victims in Kansas. The only missing element was the guerrilla perspective.[7]

Around the time Connelley began his research, Gregg, who was old, out of work, and ill, went in search of a government pension. It made no difference to Gregg that he had waged war against the government from which he now sought a pension, nor that his actions as a guerrilla were considered outside the bounds of conventional warfare and believed by many to be well beyond the limits of legally sanctioned warfare. He considered his service as legitimate as the service of any other man who fought in the war. Gregg eventually ended up in front of Harry J. Arnold, a special examiner for the Bureau of Pensions and U.S. commissioner. Although Arnold told Gregg that his chances of receiving a pension were not good, he offered an alternative avenue for financial support. While some of the details of this agreement are lost to time, he must have known that Connelley, who was also serving as a pension examiner, was looking for a guerrilla to help him write his book and that Gregg might be useful in that capacity. Arnold told Gregg that his story was worth something, and the old guerrilla, desperate for money, sold his story for the humble sum of ninety dollars. Once Gregg had written the memoir, he was "not to write another directly or indirectly."[8]

Arnold introduced Connelley to Gregg in 1902. Gregg was a godsend for Connelley, who was trying to get the inside scoop on the guerrillas and was in desperate need of credibility. For the next seven years or so, these two men corresponded with each other regularly. On the surface, their relationship was built on their tandem desire to tell the most accurate history of Quantrill and his guerrillas. It extended, however, to matters of the present. The letters seem to reveal a genuine bond of friendship. While helping Connelley with his history, Gregg also wished him luck on an oil venture, saying, "I do hope that your oil business is proving successful. If I can't be wealthy myself, I would like to see my friends get there just the same." Seemingly out of the kindness of his heart, Connelley helped Gregg find employment as a deputy sheriff in Jackson County, Missouri, and wrote a letter to the Missouri governor on

---

7. Edwards, *Noted Guerrillas*. Also see Hulbert, "Constructing Guerrilla Memory," 58–81. Some of Connelley's other books include *James Henry Lane, John Brown*, and *Wyandot Folk-Lore*.

8. Affidavit by William E. Connelley concerning the origins and ownership of the so-called Gregg Manuscript, Quantrill Collection.

Gregg's behalf, most likely in support of Gregg's application for a pension. Later, in 1909, Connelley wrote in support of Gregg's appointment as superintendent of the Confederate Home at Higginsville, Missouri.[9] What mattered most to both men, though, was the history. In his first letter to Connelley, or at least the first that has survived, Gregg demonstrated a deep concern for truth, the *objective* nature of history. He told Connelley, "There are big yarns told by both sides that, when run down to facts, many of them at least, prove to be incorrect, if not wholly false. I have had men tell of some terrible things they did in a certain battle, when I knew positively they weren't there, such men I never mentioned in my memoirs." Connelley reassured Gregg, saying of his history of the war along the Kansas-Missouri border, "I have tried to state just the facts. . . . Many of the guerrillas were needlessly brutal and murderous, but instances of kindness and manliness must be credited to even them if they did any."[10]

Gregg simultaneously helped his new friend with his book and wrote his own memoir of the war, which Connelley promised to publish. Whenever Connelley's leads dried up, he contacted Gregg, who helped him fill in the blanks. Most of their dialogue about the war was through written correspondence, but the letters allude to conversations that they had in person either in Missouri or Kansas. Eventually, Gregg completed his own memoir and sent it off to Connelley. Although his original contract had been with Arnold, Gregg was working under the assumption that Connelley owned the rights to his memoir. Documentation shows that this was not the case until 1908, when Connelley officially purchased the rights to the Gregg memoir from Arnold. Additionally, Gregg seemed to believe that his deal with Connelley was more profitable than the measly ninety dollars Arnold had promised him. In one letter Gregg told Connelley, "My friends have been clamoring at me about my little book. I have had inquiries from California, from a library in St. Louis, and many other places, besides my many friends in this and adjoining counties.

---

9. William H. Gregg to William E. Connelley, November 24, 1903; Connelley to the Governor of Missouri, August 26, 1909, Spencer Research Library, University of Kansas, Lawrence. Gregg ended up receiving an interview with the governor but never became the superintendent of the Confederate Home.

10. Gregg to Connelley, February 11, 1903; Connelley to Gregg, June 30, 1909, Quantrill Collection. The belief that an objective history was possible was very much alive at the turn of the century, even among the first professional historians in America. Since that time, the pursuit of objectivity has been discarded as an impossible venture. Novick, *That Noble Dream*.

And even Kansans have sent requests for the book when it is published." Gregg wanted to share his story and to make a bit of money in the process; he wrote to Connelley about these inquiries hoping to inspire Connelley to publish the book as he had promised.[11]

The correspondence between Gregg and Connelley is revealing of the relationship between historians and their sources. Even more than Gregg's memoir, the letters between the two men lay bare the way in which the historian worked to actively create a history of the guerrilla war in Missouri. Reading the letters from beginning to end exposes a glimpse into Connelley's thought process. revealing which parts of the history Connelley was struggling with and which pieces of information were impossible for him to ascertain without the help of an insider like Gregg. This is not unlike the way historians engage their inanimate primary sources. Historians first read what the source has to say on the surface. Then they ask questions of the source, come at it from different angles, and try to wring it dry of all information. As a source who was alive at the time of interrogation, Gregg not only answered questions but pleaded over and over again with Connelley that his history of the war not be mythology or libel. He did not want his past to be misrepresented.[12]

Between 1909 and 1910, Gregg stopped waiting for his memoir to be published. Around the same time, the correspondence between these men came to a halt, a blunt indication that their friendship had run its course. The reason for these simultaneous endings was the publication of Connelley's book on the guerrilla war, *Quantrill and the Border Wars*. Published in 1910, it revealed to Gregg that his so-called friend had deceived and used him to bring a veneer of credibility to his book while at the same time undermining the essence of Gregg's history and blocking the publication of his memoir. Connelley's book is one-sided, dedicated to the complete denunciation of Quantrill, the guerrilla war, and southern community in western Missouri, a far cry from Connelley's assurance to Gregg that he had written an evenhanded history. This all became painfully clear to Gregg as he turned to page 222 of *Quantrill and the Border Wars* and read a footnote in which Connelley claimed that he owned the

---

11. Gregg to Connelley, February 26, 1907, Quantrill Collection.

12. The Gregg-Connelley correspondence includes twenty-one surviving letters between the two men. Some of the letters are handwritten originals and some are typed—probably a mix of typed originals and transcribed copies of handwritten originals. Most of the letters are from Gregg to Connelley, which makes quite a bit of sense because the historian held onto nearly all of his documents. The original letters and transcriptions can be found in the Quantrill Collection.

"Gregg Manuscript" and that he had used the memoir throughout his research. Connelley said that the memoir is "modest and truthful" and did not have any "of the spirit of boast and brag" that accompanies so many other memoirs of the war, but the implication was clear: he never planned to publish it as a separate book. Instead, he used it to drape his own narrative in a façade of authenticity. Throughout *Quantrill and the Border Wars*, Connelley quotes, cites, and otherwise (mis)uses Gregg's memoir to such an extent that it seemed to no longer have value as a stand-alone piece. In fact, the possibility that the memoir would be published was a danger to Connelley because it contradicted many of his conclusions.[13]

Connelley's motive for deceiving Gregg and writing his own version of history grew from a particular historical and political vision of the world. Although we know little about Connelley's past, it is clear that his beliefs originated in the war, during which he was a boy growing up in a Unionist household in eastern Kentucky. Even as a child, he was likely aware of the irregular warfare that was rampant in the area and may have felt that his family was besieged by antagonistic Southerners. Sometime in the 1880s he moved to Kansas, where the local populace reinforced his radical Unionist ideas. Connelley was a partisan who saw history as his battleground, a place to fight for just, moral, and right causes with little concern for accuracy or empathy. Books were the weapons used to wage this war. Just as his politics made it impossible to see anything but evil in Quantrill, slaveholding Missourians, or anyone else who lined up against the Union, Kansas, and the abolitionist cause, Connelley's worldview made it easy to rationalize deceiving a man he called a friend. That friendship was merely collateral damage necessary to win the war for history.[14]

For more than four decades, *Quantrill and the Border Wars* was the standard text for anyone interested in Missouri guerrillas, the war along the state's western border, and Quantrill. Then, in 1958, Richard S. Brownlee published *Gray Ghosts of the Confederacy*, the first such work by a pro-

---

13. Connelley, *Quantrill and the Border Wars*, 222.
14. For the best look at the way in which the guerrilla war was waged in Appalachia, see McKnight, *Confederate Outlaw*. Additionally, For specific mentions of Johnson County, Kentucky, see McKnight, *Contested Borderland*, 89, 98, 156, and 192. For a description of internal divisions in a community similar to the one in which Connelley grew up, see Mann, "Ezekiel Counts's Sand Lick Company: Civil War and Localism in the Mountain South," in *The Civil War in Appalachia: Collected Essays*, ed. Kenneth W. Noe and Shannon H. Wilson (Knoxville: University of Tennessee Press, 1997), 78–103.

For background on Connelley, see Beilein and Hulbert, *The Civil War Guerrilla*, 207–30.

fessional scholar on the war in western Missouri and an upgrade in scholarship quality from *Quantrill and the Border Wars*. Even with his success in writing about the guerrillas, Connelley was finished with them and their war. He seemed to move on with ease, putting it all behind him. Ironically, for the man who thought of himself as a scholar with broad interests—the history of the guerrillas formed just a small part of his career—it was his connection to the guerrilla war in Missouri for which he is most remembered. Indeed, *Quantrill and the Border Wars* left a lasting impression on the field of Civil War–era guerrilla studies, an influence that is quite obvious in modern works on the subject.[15]

Unlike Connelley, Gregg was unable to move on from the war. The war was not a pet project; it was a fundamental part of his life. The once even-tempered Gregg began to push a more militant, reactionary narrative of the war that stood in stark contrast to Connelley's book. Connelley once said of Gregg that "when the war was over it was over forever with Captain Gregg, and he immediately returned to his farm and took up the pursuits of peace, which he ever after cherished and followed." Gregg's own letters from the period before *Quantrill and the Border Wars* also indicated that he wanted to reconcile with his former adversaries. After the book's publication and the revelation of its author's deception, Gregg began to say things like "We went there to burn and kill and we did it" when he talked about the raid on Lawrence. He was unrepentant, a rebel, and he wanted everyone to know it. More than that, he wanted them to know that he and his cohort were right. Whether he forgot about the contract that precluded him from sharing his story or just did not care, Gregg began to speak at reunions and to newspaper reporters, his tongue cutting with a razor-sharp edge.[16]

The Guerrilla War in Missouri

Gregg's experience in guerrilla warfare was a product of the particular local conditions in western Missouri. In October 1861 Andrew Walker—the son of a wealthy Jackson County, Missouri, farmer—formed a neighborhood patrol to defend slaveholders from raiding jayhawkers. This patrol, which was composed of Walker and his brother, a few local boys, and

---

15. Brownlee, *Gray Ghosts of the Confederacy*.
16. Connelley, *Quantrill and the Border Wars*, 222. *Confederate Veteran*, May 1907, 279; *Kansas City Times*, August 20, 1910.

State of Missouri, 1861-1865

Railroads

Major Rivers

Counties

0 15 30 60 90 120 Miles

N

Counties of Missouri.
Courtesy of Andrew Fialka.

Quantrill, was the prototype for the guerrilla bands that soon popped up across the state. As Walker remembered, his patrol skirmished with Union troopers who were abusing Southern sympathizers in his neighborhood, killing one of the soldiers. Later, as the need for the patrol became permanent, Walker went back to his farm and left Quantrill in charge. With eight men, Quantrill tried to protect Southerners from the encroachment of Union occupation troops, many of whom were from Kansas or rode alongside jayhawkers.[17]

The early days of guerrilla fighting took on the character of raid and counterraid. A steady influx of Union troops into Jackson County forced the guerrillas off the country roads and into the brush, where they spent much of the rest of the war hiding out from enemy patrols. When the countryside was clear, they attacked weakly or completely undefended Union outposts or ambushed small, vulnerable Union units. Likewise, the Union army tried to catch the guerrillas unaware in a brushy campsite or napping in the home of a supporter. Compared with what the war in Missouri became, this time in the conflict had an almost romantic quality. Each side took prisoners and exchanged them; enemies treated each other nobly.[18]

In March 1862, the dynamics of the guerrilla war in Missouri changed. Henry Halleck, the general commanding the Department of the Missouri, was fed up with guerrillas, their hit-and-run raids, and their unwillingness to come out of the brush and line up and fight like real men. The problem Halleck faced was not limited to Quantrill's band in western Missouri; the whole state was alive with Southern-sympathizing guerrillas. To put a stop to this warfare, which he believed was unlawful, he outlawed guerrilla tactics, putting guerrillas in the same category as spies and pirates. Without the protections afforded lawful combatants, the guerrillas faced execution when captured. Instead of discouraging men from fighting as guerrillas, Halleck's draconian measures only made matters worse, and more Southern men took to the brush to retaliate.[19]

---

17. Walker, *Recollections of Quantrill's Guerrillas.* Walker was probably the closest man to Quantrill, at least before the war and in its earliest days. Combined, the Walker and Gregg memoirs offer the best portrait of Quantrill up to the winter of 1863–64, when the band disintegrated.

18. For an introduction into the history of the guerrilla war, see Brownlee, *Gray Ghosts of the Confederacy.*

19. *The War of the Rebellion: A Compilation of the Official Records of the Union and Confederate Armies* (hereafter cited as O.R.), series 1, vol. 8, part 1, 463–64, 611–12.

District of the Border
June 9, 1863

| Washington | Marshall | Nemaha | Brown | Doniphan |

Atchison

Atchison

Fort Leavenworth

| Clay | Riley | Pottawatomie | Jackson |

Jefferson · Leavenworth · Lexington

Topeka · Kansas City · Wyandotte · Lafayette

| Davis | Wabaunsee | Shawnee | Lawrence · Independence · Blue Springs |

Olathe · Jackson · Lone Jack

| Dickinson | | | Douglas | Johnson | Johnson · Warrensburg |

| Morris | Osage | Harrisonville |

Cass/Van Buren

Breckinridge · Franklin · Miami/Lykins

| Marion | Chase | | | | Clinton |

| | | Coffey | Anderson | Linn | Bates · Butler · Henry/Rives |

Madison

Osceola

Butler · St Clair

| Otoe | | | | | |

| Greenwood | Woodson | Allen | Bourbon | Vernon |

KANSAS   MISSOURI

- Cities
— State Line
= Missouri River
▬ 38th Parallel
▨ Area Subject to Order No. 11
☐ County

N
▲

Union-occupied district of the border where William H. Gregg
and his cohort primarily fought their guerrilla war.
Courtesy of Andrew Fialka.

With support from their families, the guerrillas waged a successful war against their enemies in western Missouri. In some ways the opening act of the guerrilla war in Missouri paralleled the opening stages of guerrilla movements across the South, both Confederate and Unionist. Whether they were Southern-sympathizing communities along the border responding to Union invasion or Unionists in Appalachia or even in the Mississippi hinterlands, local communities often looked inward for military identity and organization. By its very nature the guerrilla war was fought around the guerrillas' homes, making it gender inclusive, with women playing a direct role. Women were the logistical backbone of the guerrilla war effort, supplying the guerrillas with food, clothing, ammunition, powder, animals, information, and anything else they could to help their men in the brush.[20]

In Missouri this gender dynamic played a defining role in the increasing trajectory of violence over the course of the war. Although the men who went into the brush adjusted to the Union's hard war policies to protect themselves, their households were vulnerable to attack, which put the guerrillas' loved ones and their war at risk. As it became more obvious to the Union that they could not catch the men they wanted to kill, they began to target guerrilla households and guerrilla women. When their homes were attacked, the guerrillas lost the people they loved, and the foundation of their war effort crumbled.[21]

In the summer of 1863, a series of household-centered events occurred that changed the landscape of the guerrilla war in Missouri yet again. Under the astute leadership of Brigadier General Thomas Ewing, Union soldiers in the District of the Border began to identify, pursue, arrest, and imprison the mothers, sisters, and sweethearts of the guerrillas as a matter of formal policy. Some of these women were arrested and imprisoned in the newly minted women's prison, a shaky row house in downtown Kansas City. The haphazard prison was accidentally undermined when Union soldiers pulled out a load-bearing pillar from the basement of the house next door to make room for barracks. Because the two homes shared a wall, the weakened foundation of the one house pulled them both down. Several of the female prisoners were killed outright, and the others were badly injured. Although it was unintentional, the guerrillas just assumed

---

20. For an in-depth look into household war see Beilein, *Bushwhackers*.
21. Ibid.

the collapse had been orchestrated on purpose to kill their loved ones. After all, the guerrillas believed their Union enemies had changed the rules of war to suit their own needs, twice: first when they began executing guerrillas and second when they began targeting households. If Union soldiers would shoot prisoners and torch their homes, then what kept them from escalating things further by killing their wives and sweethearts?[22]

The collapse of the women's prison influenced the violence the guerrillas let loose in the raid on Lawrence, Kansas, on August 21, 1863. Although it was the Union's systematic onslaught against the Southern households that led Quantrill to plan the raid, the death of the guerrilla women enraged many of the men beyond self-restraint. William Anderson, who had one sister killed in the prison collapse and two others maimed, went on a rampage at Lawrence, killing as many as fourteen men and earning his fearful sobriquet "Bloody Bill" likely in the wake of his excessive bloodletting there. Although no one matched Anderson for the toll he took on the people of Lawrence, the other men who did more than their share of killing were likely related to the crushed women. In total, Quantrill's 400 or so raiders killed around 180 mostly unarmed men and boys and burned nearly the entire settlement to the ground before making their getaway.[23]

This attack on Northern households at Lawrence prompted an extreme reaction from Union forces. While jayhawkers had been attacking Southern households since before the war and soldiers assigned to the District of the Border had been trying to cut out individual households as a part of their guerrilla containment strategy, Union forces now razed the entire Southern community along the border. Ewing, who was feeling pressure from all sides because the raid on Lawrence had occurred on his watch, proclaimed General Order 11, which stated that "all persons living in Jackson, Cass, and Bates counties, Missouri, and in that part of Vernon included in this district, except those living within one mile of the limits of Independence, Hickman's Mills, Pleasant Hill, and Harrisonville, and except those in that part of Kaw Township, Jackson County, north of Brush Creek and west of Big Blue, are hereby ordered to remove from their present places of residence within fifteen days from the date hereof." After two weeks, Union troopers enforced the order with prej-

---

22. Whites, "Forty Shirts," 56–78.
23. Harris, "Catalyst for Terror," 290–306.

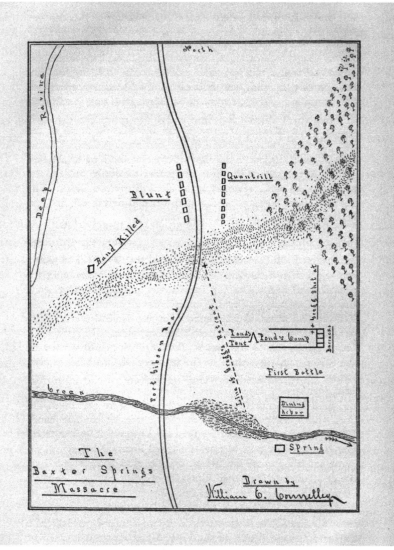

Connelley drew this map of Baxter Springs
after close consultation with Gregg.
From Connelley, *Quantrill and the Border Wars*, 426.

udice, booting nearly every family in the four counties, torching their fields, storehouses, barns, and houses, and killing every military-age man with Southern sympathies who was foolish enough to remain at home. The Missouri side of the border, once the site of fertile fields, lush forests, and expansive farms and plantations, was turned into a barren stretch known for years afterwards as the Burnt District.[24]

After the prison collapse, the Lawrence raid, and General Order 11, the guerrillas headed south to Texas for the winter in October 1863. On their way, leaders of Quantrill's guerrilla army found a Union outpost known as Fort Blair at Baxter Springs, Kansas. Under the leadership of William Gregg and Dave Pool, some of the guerrillas assaulted the fort but were driven back. Just moments later, the rest of Quantrill's men, who were rushing to the sound of gunfire for a chance to get in on the fight, smashed into a column of Union troopers traveling to Fort Blair. More than one hundred of the Union troopers in the column were killed— nearly the entire command. In the wake of this slaughter, the entire force of guerrillas turned their horses toward Fort Blair. Quantrill reconnoitered the fort and decided another attack on the entrenched troopers would be disastrous for his men. His decision not to attack planted a seed of mutiny in the hearts of some of his officers that quickly grew into a thorny weed of dissension.[25]

After a few months in Texas, tensions rose among individuals and the various factions of guerrillas. It was an unprecedented feat for one leader to keep hundreds of guerrillas together as long as Quantrill managed to. In Missouri's guerrilla war, men typically rode in bands of ten or so, a practical necessity, as most farm households were capable of feeding around ten men; more than that strained a family supporting the war. Each band was led by a guerrilla captain who attained his position through his charisma, leadership, fighting skills, and his standing in the antebellum community. Men like Bloody Bill Anderson and George Todd began to chafe under Quantrill's leadership. Likewise, self-selecting groups of men began to fall into different "camps" of drinkers and non-drinkers, wild men and men of self-discipline, Jackson County men and those from areas near the border. With so much idle time, the rivalries that had been suppressed during the hard fighting days began to rear their heads in the saloons and streets of Sherman, Texas, and factions

24. *O.R.*, series 1, vol. 22, part 2, 428.
25. Castel and Goodrich, *Bloody Bill Anderson*, 31–33.

began to split off. Anderson left with a large number of fighters. As the rest of the group traveled back to Missouri, Todd humiliated Quantrill in a card game, and the two split. The majority of the band took off with Todd. This was the end of Quantrill's raiders.[26]

It was not, however, the end of the guerrilla war in Missouri. Not only did the conflict continue, but it took on new forms; indeed, the summer of 1864 proved to be the bloodiest yet for the guerrillas. Bloody Bill Anderson and his cohort of killers became infamous across the state for slaughtering their enemies in ambushes and raids. Now, for the first time, scalping and other forms of mutilation became standard elements of guerrilla violence. This bloody summer drew to a fitting end at Centralia, Missouri, on September 27. Anderson's guerrillas turned the streets of that country town into a carnival of blood when they executed twenty-two unarmed Union soldiers. Later that day, the same guerrillas, bolstered by two or three hundred others from another half-dozen guerrilla bands, ambushed a Union patrol of 130 men that came after them, killing all but a handful of the troopers. Afterward, the guerrillas went to work with their knives, taking scalps—per usual—but also removing noses, fingers, genitals, heads, and any other body parts that might make suitable trophies.[27]

The war ended in its own way for each guerrilla. Some guerrillas went with Quantrill to Kentucky and carried on into the summer of 1865, when their commander died and they surrendered. Many men kept up the fight across the state and surrendered at places like Lexington or the Boone County fairgrounds. Quite a few guerrillas died at the hands of Union troopers or pro-Union militiamen. By the summer of 1865, the majority of the guerrillas who were still alive came in from the brush, though a few, such as Jesse James, never came in at all.[28]

Gregg's War and Memoir

It is easy to understand why Gregg thought it so important to capture the war as he saw it in his memoir. His correspondence implies that he prob-

26. Castel and Goodrich, *Bloody Bill Anderson*, 33–36; Connelley, *Quantrill and the Border Wars*, 444–47.

27. *O.R.*, series 1, vol. 41, part 1, 440–41.

28. James claimed that he had tried to come in and surrender but was ambushed rather than given the amnesty promised to the guerrillas. See Stiles, *Jesse James*, 153–55.

ably finished the memoir, which was a little more than a hundred pages, in less than two years, but the State Historical Society of Missouri asserts that he completed it in 1906. After Connelley's deception, Gregg feared that his memoir would never be published. However, although Connelley may have intended never to publish it, ever the historian, he did not destroy or discard it. Somehow it ended up in the hands of B. J. George Sr., an amateur historian, collector, and descendant of a Missouri guerrilla, or in the hands of Frank Glenn, a bookseller in Kansas City. The State Historical Society of Missouri attributes ownership of the memoir to both men. Somehow, one of them secured the memoir in its original handwritten form, and a copy eventually made its way to the State Historical Society of Missouri.[29]

Gregg's recollection of the war offers significant insight into the guerrilla conflict and challenges the traditional understanding of the war. After the end of the Civil War, the guerrilla war became a mostly forgotten sideshow or was considered an arena of outlaws, brigands, and other ne'er-do-wells of the mid-nineteenth century. The guerrilla war has always been the *other*, something alien when compared with the *real* Civil War. When Gregg was writing his memoir, he thought few people in the country knew much at all about the guerrillas or properly understood them. For example, even after all of their dialogue, Connelley emphasized the horrid nature of the guerrilla war as something distinct from the rest of the Civil War. According to Connelley, "In wealth of romantic incidents, stirring adventures, hair-breadth escapes, sanguinary ambuscades, deadly encounters, individual vengeance, relentless desolation of towns and communities, and bloody murder, no other part of America can compare with it." Even now, the most popular historical views of the guerrilla war echo Connelley's description: one well-known historian of the guerrilla war has described it as a war of "a thousand nasty incidents." Even more recently, scholars who focus on aspects of the war that fall within the bounds of traditional military history have claimed that the conventional war waged on conventional battlefields by men in uniform was the *real* war. Given the tone of these recent arguments, it seems they

---

29. According to the State Historical Society of Missouri's card catalog, the Gregg Manuscript was purchased from Frank Glenn, a bookseller in Kansas City, Missouri, on July 23, 1943. The front matter of the actual Gregg memoir, however, states "B.J. George, Sr. Collections." B. J. George Sr. was born in 1887. He had relatives among the guerrillas and attended their reunions as a boy and young man. It is quite likely that he knew Gregg.

actually believe it was the *only* war. For Gregg, though, the guerrilla war was *the* war, as legitimate and as real as any other part of the conflict.[30]

Gregg clearly thought his time as a guerrilla was more significant than his experience in the formal Confederate army. Although he spent the final year and a half of the war serving as a regular in General Jo Shelby's cavalry, Gregg wrote about fighting alongside Quantrill; to him it was the most poignant part of his wartime recollections and his most important contribution to posterity. Gregg narrated, sometimes in the third person, his experiences in the war, from his joining up with Quantrill in 1861 through a series of skirmishes until Gregg left the band in early 1864. He himself was the main subject of his recollections, and he took special interest in the most controversial parts of the war. For example, the raid on Lawrence, its lead-up, planning, and fallout, provided the centerpiece for the memoir. His memoir was not just a running description of the war; Gregg offered insight into the character of the men involved and the dynamics between fighters in Quantrill's band. He sprinkled in humorous anecdotes and morality tales here and there, and he supplemented the memoir with a few stories he remembered after he had completed a draft of his recollections for Connelley. Gregg went through the memoir and marked the various places where he thought the supplemental parts of the narrative might be inserted. At times the guerrilla editorialized on subjects such as Kansans, jayhawkers, and newspapers, revealing his inner thoughts and feelings.

Gregg's memoir begins with his going into the brush. Along with James Hendricks and John Koger, he joined Quantrill and his small band on Christmas Day 1861. Gregg writes of the group as "the greatest guerrilla band the world ever produced." It was not long before Gregg rose through the ranks and became the man who was closest to Quantrill. He filled two significant positions in the band: he was elected by the men to be one of Captain Quantrill's lieutenants, leading the men in combat, and he also acted as Quantrill's de facto chief of staff. In the latter capacity, he helped his commander issue orders and acted as his agent, carrying out special missions not entrusted to any other officer. At times Gregg was Quantrill's confidant. When he was not helping to make decisions that shaped the war, he was witness to the decision-making process.

---

30. Connelley, *Quantrill and the Border Wars*, 5; Fellman, *Inside War*, 176. For a recent publication arguing for the relevance of military history, not through a sort of compromise or negotiation as their title suggests but instead mostly through attacks on other fields of study, see Gallagher and Meier, "Coming to Terms," 487–508.

Gregg's decision to join the guerrillas was informed by his past, his race, and his social class. Like most of the other men who became guerrillas, he was young. Although he was slightly older than the average guerrilla in the band, Gregg was only twenty-three when the war began. Also like his fellow guerrillas, he was born and raised in a slaveholding household. His father, Jacob Gregg, owned four slaves in 1860, and William considered whites superior to their enslaved blacks. Furthermore, the Greggs had a vested interest in the success of the South and of the proslavery cause. They were quite wealthy, with Jacob Gregg possessing nearly fifteen thousand dollars of real and personal estate. From Gregg's perspective, it made sense to go out and fight in defense of the institution of slavery and of white supremacy.[31]

Although Gregg's motivations to fight mirrored those of the men who joined the formal armies of the Confederacy, his decision to wage war as a guerrilla was influenced by factors that did not exist everywhere in the South. Geography played a critical role in a young man's choice to "go guerrilla" in western Missouri. For years, Missourians had been dealing with an enemy at their gates. Jayhawking Kansans frequently raided farms and plantations, liberated slaves, destroyed property, and killed white men and women, and the Missourians needed vigilance and armed defense. In months and years before the pitched violence of the Civil War guerrilla conflict, local patrols were established to protect the human property of white southerners, and these patrols easily transitioned into guerrilla bands, thus creating an accessible, if alternative, form of military service for young men in the area. Additionally, the entire state was experiencing a military vacuum by the winter of 1861–62. Despite a major victory at Wilson's Creek and a few minor victories, Confederate forces receded into northern Arkansas, leaving the guerrillas to defend Missouri. In Missouri, for a man like Gregg to defend his home—whether that meant his family, household, neighborhood, property in slaves, or his state—he had to go into the brush.

Gregg's decision to fight as a guerrilla was also informed by his sense of manhood. Gregg, like the other members of his bushwhacking cohort, believed it was his duty to fight when the war came along. War provided men with an opportunity to demonstrate masculine prowess, to test themselves, and to dominate other men. The bush was an especially

---

31. 1860 Federal Manuscript Census, Jackson County, Mo.; Bowen, "Guerrilla War in Western Missouri," 30–51.

attractive arena for waging war in a way that reaffirmed the masculine values held up by young white men from Missouri. They did not sacrifice their autonomy and were not subjected to the bondage of the formal, conventional armies. Instead, the war they waged emphasized freedom, individual liberty, and masculine independence. Their horses, their "irregular" dress, their revolvers, and their households all contributed to each man's independence and the primacy of the individual as the basic unit of organization within the guerrilla ranks. If a man were to fight, this was the way to do it.[32]

Gregg and his guerrilla brethren viewed the application of no-quarter by their enemies through this gendered lens. Gregg recalled in his memoir the exact sequence of events that led to a war measured by bloodshed. The guerrillas heard of Halleck's no-quarter declaration through the newspaper, but they did not immediately retaliate. Instead, they tried to wage war as they had. Their old approach proved impossible to continue, but Gregg and his cohort did not flinch when confronted with the redefined parameters of guerrilla warfare. Rather than sit passively in the brush and let Halleck dictate the new rules of war, the guerrillas met his challenge. When guerrilla Perry Hoy was captured and then executed in keeping with Halleck's policy, Quantrill executed the Union soldiers his guerrillas were holding prisoner. Then he, Gregg, and the others went into Kansas and killed ten men. Written in blood, the message they were sending to their Union enemies was clear: the guerrillas would not be cowed, intimidated into leaving the state, or baited into fighting a conventional "stand-up" war against a bigger, stronger opponent. For the most part, this was the new normal of the guerrilla war, not just for Quantrill's guerrillas nor for guerrillas in the state of Missouri, but for guerrillas across the South. These men were the first to feel the sting of the hard hand of war and the first to strike back at the Union's hard war policies.[33]

Gregg recounted a number of skirmishes that occurred in 1862 and early 1863 under the new terms of engagement. He wrote quite candidly

---

32. Beilein, *Bushwhackers*. Studies of manhood have greatly contributed to our understanding of why men fought in the Civil War. For a survey of some of the most important works in this field, see Whites, *The Civil War as a Crisis*; Silber, *The Romance of Reunion*; Berry, *All that Makes a Man*; Greenberg, *Manifest Manhood*; Foote, *The Gentlemen and the Roughs*; Miller, *John Bell Hood*.

33. Fellman, *Inside War*, 253.

about the Union's gaining the upper hand on the guerrillas from time to time, whether by surprising the guerrillas at the Tate house or during the bushwhackers' failed attempt to take the town of Independence, Missouri, in February 1862. In fact, Gregg's recollection of this part of the war was more about escaping or dodging open combat with Union troopers than it was about attacking and defeating his enemies. For the guerrillas, running was as much a part of their fight as killing. They would not sacrifice themselves; their survival was the key factor in their success. Although they were killers, and quite proud of their ability to do harm, killing was much less important than not being killed. Indeed, a certain pride comes through in Gregg's writing when he discussed their dashing escapes.[34]

Gregg mentioned two events during this period when he personally led the offensive against Union targets. In both instances, he downplayed the amount and types of violence unleashed on his enemies. First, Gregg proudly touted the destruction of the boat *Sam Gaty* under his leadership upon his return to the Missouri River valley on March 28, 1863. While he listed the half a million dollars' worth of items destroyed by him and his men—"sugar, coffee, bacon"—and said they had killed fourteen soldiers in the fight, Gregg failed to mention the nine to twenty black men they had killed. Union reports implied that these men were executed in an act of racial vengeance, an act that was unfortunately common in the Civil War but that was apparently too unsavory and shameful for Gregg to confess at the turn of the century. Silence on this issue raises questions about other parts of the manuscript; Gregg may have omitted unflattering events in which he participated.[35]

Gregg also neglected to mention the more extreme acts of violence he and his men carried out against white men. While it is important to remember that Gregg left the guerrilla war before scalping and most of the mutilation began, he was nevertheless party to some nasty bloodletting. During the summer of 1863, Gregg led an ambush against a Union patrol. A guerrilla supporter pretending to be a Union man reported drunk bushwhackers at his residence to lure the militia unit, led by a Captain Sessions, out into the countryside to a killing zone Gregg had selected. After the Union troopers rode out, the guerrillas went to work.

---

34. For analysis of the significance of running and hiding to guerrilla identity, see Beilein, *Bushwhackers*, 215–41.

35. *O.R.*, series 1, vol. 22, part 1, 245–46; part 2, 183, 194–95, 203.

Gregg was quite vague in his account of the attack, leaving the reader to assume that Sessions and all of his men were shot down during the fight. This could certainly be true, but it was unlikely. A Union report painted a rather different picture, in which only a few of the men, including Sessions, were shot off their horses during the ambush. However, in this telling, the guerrillas emerged from their brushy hiding spots to finish the wounded men off with shots to the head. The Union report said that Sessions was shot several times in the head, an overkill that seemed more postmortem mutilation than battlefield wound.[36]

Eventually, the guerrillas as a whole went on the offensive. Gregg's account of the planning of the Lawrence raid confirmed that although the prison collapse inspired anger, it did not cause the raid. Rather, the raid was in the planning stages before the collapse took place. Gregg remembered that Quantrill brought his commanders together on August 10, 1863—three days before the walls of the makeshift penitentiary came down on the heads of those guerrilla women—to propose his plan to attack "the great hotbed of abolitionism in Kansas." According to Gregg the cause of the raid was that jayhawkers, who were now raiding under the authority of the United States, were becoming more pervasive in their assaults on Southern households. According to his recollection, they were "murdering, plundering and devastating the houses of a greater or less number of our citizens, and to kill, it was only necessary to know that a man sympathized with the South, but, as to robbing, they robbed everyone without distinction, and they often laid waste to whole districts."

Gregg offered evidence that the raid was an appropriate act in the context of household war as the guerrillas understood it. Without exception, the guerrillas who participated in the Lawrence raid and later spoke or wrote about it were proud of their actions. Most of the guerrillas used emotional language to explain why such a raid was just, blaming the people of Lawrence for the attack: *they* killed my father; *they* burned down my home; *they* assaulted my mother. However, Gregg argued that the guerrilla assault made sense in the context of a systematic household war. As the raid neared its conclusion in the streets of Lawrence, Gregg was sent by Quantrill to round the men up for departure. While riding around town, he found shanties filled to the rafters with loot from Missouri, guarded by black women who were once enslaved by white Missourians. Before leaving, the guerrillas did their best to gather up what they

---

36. *O.R.*, series 1, vol. 22, part 1, 335–36.

could, pile it on wagons and throw it in saddle bags, and haul it back to their supporters on the other side of the border. Gregg's discovery of the stolen loot and liberated black women confirmed Quantrill's claim that the people of Lawrence benefited from the violence directed at Southern households and Gregg's opinion that the raid was not simply a slaughter of innocents but an attempt to recoup household goods.[37]

Although Gregg did not speak to the fate of the women he found with the stolen goods from Missouri, it was unlikely that he omitted mention of racially charged violence as he had in his account of the attack on the *Sam Gaty*. Unlike the attack on the riverboat, in which other pieces of primary evidence suggested Gregg's whitewashing of the event, no such evidence exists here. The pro-Union sources in Lawrence do not speak to the murder of black women. They confirm that the guerrillas targeted unarmed men and boys—white and black—and that they killed them in horrific ways. There is no mention, however, of any women being killed.[38]

After the raid on Lawrence, Gregg witnessed the disintegration of Quantrill's raiders. From early on in the war, some of the men fighting in the brush were more thoughtful about their tactics in fighting Union troopers and were more reserved in terms of their violence than others. Gregg and Quantrill were among the more conservative. That does not mean that they were not killers; they waged a war of no-quarter as did all of the other guerrillas. However, they were not as eager to kill or as reckless with their own lives as men like George Todd or Bloody Bill Anderson, who Quantrill constantly reined in. When the guerrillas began to move southward in the fall of 1863, each member under Quantrill's command was being pulled toward one extreme or the other.[39]

---

37. McCorkle, *Three Years with Quantrill*, 122–23; Harris, "Catalyst for Terror," 290–306.

38. Reverend Richard Cordley's letter to congress about the raid on Lawrence is the most thorough account of the event at "The Lawrence Massacre by a Band of Missouri Ruffians under Quantrill," Kansas Collection Books, June 30, 1994, http://www.kancoll. org/books/cordley_massacre/quantrel.raid.html.

39. All of the memoirs and recollections that speak about it claim that the guerrillas observed the ancient rules of war as they understood them, taking prisoners and paroling or exchanging them until Halleck's no-quarter orders took hold. Union reports did not make any claims to the contrary. Scalping and the most extreme forms of violence do not make an appearance in most of the guerrilla recollections until 1863 at the earliest. Documents in the *O.R.* do not say anything about scalping until 1864. By then Quantrill was out of power, and some of the original men like Gregg were gone. See Beilein, *Bushwhackers*, 165– 88. Also see Beilein, "Whiskey and the War: Alcohol, Violence, and Guerrillas in Civil War Missouri," in *The Guerrilla Hunters: Irregular Conflicts during the Civil War*, ed. Barton A. Myers and Brian D. McKnight (Baton Rouge: Louisiana State University Press, 2017), 236–59.

The band began to break apart at Baxter Springs. Gregg was standing by when "Todd and Anderson both insisted that we should storm and take the fort" and no doubt observed their visible disdain when Quantrill denied them the morbid pleasure of charging headlong at the well-defended fortification. Before this rebuke, Gregg experienced firsthand the tension between Quantrill and his two most notable subordinates. Quantrill sent Gregg to discipline Anderson for stealing horses in 1862, and he watched Todd and Quantrill nearly come to blows, likely a couple of times. It was only a matter of time before Anderson and Todd broke off from the band. For his own part, Gregg cut ties with the guerrillas in Texas during the winter of 1863–64, deciding instead to join the formal Confederate army. Although he did not give his reasons, it seems likely that death threats from other men in the group, who were upset with Gregg because he had reported them as thieves, pushed him to leave Quantrill's band. Not long after Gregg left, Anderson tried to frame Quantrill for murder, then rode off with a large number of men. On the way back from Texas, Todd usurped Quantrill after a card game gone awry and took command of most of the band.[40]

Gregg made one more cameo in the guerrilla war. Although he left the guerrillas to join the formal ranks of the Confederate army, the force he joined allowed him to visit his old stomping ground. Shelby's cavalry force raided into Missouri in 1864 along with the rest of Sterling Price's army of Missourians. Price, one-time governor of the state and Confederate general, made a desperate attempt to retake Missouri and ultimately failed. During the campaign, Price provided quite a bit of freedom to his officers, especially when they were close to home. Gregg used this freedom to remove his sweetheart from the war zone. In the fall of 1864, Gregg asked Lizzie Hook to marry him. When she said "yes," Gregg rounded up many of his old bushwhacking comrades and rode over to the Hook household, where a guerrilla wedding took place. Then, after the nuptials, the bride and groom, along with two other couples and around forty guerrillas, rode south to Texas, where Gregg set up his wife far from the reach of the war.[41]

---

40. William E. Connelley, Interview with William H. Gregg, July 14, 1916, William E. Connelley Collection, RH MS 2, Box 1, Spencer Research Library, University of Kansas, Lawrence.

41. Lizzie Gregg, "Can Forgive, but Never Forget," in *Reminiscences of the Women of Missouri during the Sixties*, comp. United Daughters of the Confederacy, Missouri Division (Dayton: Morningside Press, 1988), 29–30.

William Clarke Quantrill

Throughout his memoir, Gregg offered quite a bit of insight into the life of his leader. His observations, along with those of Andrew Walker and Quantrill's bride, Kate Clark, offer the best description of Quantrill and the most accurate rendering of his thoughts and actions. That said, Quantrill was a mystery then and continues to be enigmatic. A couple of major questions about the guerrilla chief remain unanswered: Why did his political views shift from anti- to proslavery? Why did he betray his jayhawker cohort at the Walker farm? Likely there will never be enough evidence to answer these questions to the satisfaction of professional historians. Rather than speculate, it is perhaps better to think about a few questions that are even more important: Why would a slaveholding community adopt this outsider who originally came to them as a jayhawker? And why did they trust him to fight for them so much that he eventually became the most powerful man in their guerrilla war? To understand Quantrill, one must shift focus from the individual to the institutions, communities, and happenings of the world in which he lived and fought.

By all accounts, including Gregg's, Quantrill cut a striking figure. He was thin but strong, standing just under six feet tall, with a straight back and broad shoulders. His hair, at least at the outset of the war, was so blond that it was nearly white, causing Gregg to refer to Quantrill as a tow-head. Quantrill's beard, though, took on a reddish hue. Andrew Walker remembered Quantrill as having a small "Roman" nose that Connelley described as "sinister" looking. Gregg said that Quantrill's eyes were blueish-gray; most who knew the guerrilla chieftain and left a record of their observations noted his strange eyes. Walker said that Quantrill had the "brightest, most remarkable eyes you would find in a lifetime." At different points in his life, both before and during the war, Quantrill donned a bright red flannel shirt. All of this together made for an unforgettable man: a shock of white hair, a red mustache and beard, and electric blue eyes, wrapped up in bright red flannel. The sight was enough to spark an instant visceral reaction to the man's character. As Connelley said, "With some people he was in great good repute, while others despised him from first sight without being able to explain why."[42]

---

42. Walker, *Recollections of Quantrill's Guerrillas*, 2; Connelley, *Quantrill and the Border Wars*, 43.

William C. Quantrill.
Frontispiece from Connelley,
Quantrill and the Border Wars.

This striking figure had a mysterious and misunderstood backstory. Some time after they met in December 1861, Quantrill told Gregg the same story about his background that he had been telling Missourians for a year. Quantrill had appeared twelve months earlier at the Morgan Walker farm in Jackson County, Missouri. He revealed himself to be in the company of several men from Kansas—jayhawkers—who wished to do the Walker clan harm by stealing (or liberating) their slaves, taking their money, and killing them. These men had been Quantrill's associates. There is no real indication why he decided to turn on them at that moment or what, if any, jayhawking he had participated in. His betrayal of the jayhawkers allowed the Walkers to ambush them, killing one man outright and killing the other two a couple days later in the brush. After the initial ambush, Quantrill told the Walkers two lies: that the men he betrayed had murdered his brother and this was his final act of revenge and that he hailed from the slave state of Maryland. The origins of the second lie are clear enough. Now that he found himself in a Southern community surrounded by men and women with extreme proslavery politics who were more skeptical than ever of outsiders, Quantrill was trying to assuage any fears and save his neck from the lynch mob's noose. The first lie is harder to decipher. Quantrill had a brother, but he was much younger and never was in Kansas, let alone killed by jayhawkers.[43]

As elusive as Quantrill is, several parts of his life are well established. He was born in Canal Dover, Ohio, in 1837 and raised in a household that was in step with the political and cultural trends of that place and time. That is to say, the proslavery politics he later defended as a guerrilla were vastly different from the worldview in which he was brought up. Quantrill became the oldest male in his household when his father, a somewhat learned man, a tinker, and also a schoolmaster, died in the 1850s. Obviously smart, Quantrill became a teacher as a teenager and taught children in his hometown. Like the thousands of other young men of the era, Quantrill felt the itch to move westward to make his fortune, or at least a life for himself. He left home for Illinois in the mid-1850s but only stayed for a few months. After returning home for a short while, he moved to Kansas Territory with some men from his hometown. After a disagreement with these men over money and landownership, Quantrill moved on to find work. He became a teamster and tried his hand at mining while in the far West, but he eventually returned to Kansas and to teaching. Then, all of a sudden, he was caught up in the sectional conflict that drew in so many young men along the border. He likely participated in the informal war across the border between Kansas Territory and Missouri, but exactly how and for how long remains obscure. Then he appeared at the Walker farm in December 1860.[44]

Gregg rode a fine line when discussing Quantrill's past, offering no definitive statement about the veracity of his captain's personal history. Nor did he make any judgment. Instead, Gregg negotiated Quantrill's backstory like a well-trained documentarian. He told the reader, "Quantrill, (his story to the contrary notwithstanding) was born at Canal Dover, Ohio, at least, a woman said to be his mother, says he was born there." Then in the very next paragraph, Gregg said, "Quantrill told me this story," then repeated the backstory that Quantrill constructed as a way of ingratiating himself into the Southern community of Jackson County. Although Gregg presented both sides—the truth and the lie—it was ev-

---

43. Walker, *Recollections of Quantrill's Guerrillas*, 1–4.
44. Connelley, *Quantrill and the Border Wars*, 29, 42–53, 62–102.

ident that Gregg was brought in like the other men by Quantrill's fabricated backstory. He wanted to believe that his leader was a Southerner and that he was some vengeful warrior.

Quantrill began his rise to prominence approximately one year after his arrival in Missouri. After the ambush at the Walker farm, he stayed with the Walker family in the capacity of a hired hand, but he became close with them, even befriending Andrew Walker. Eventually, Quantrill was loaned out to a man named Marcus Gill—a friend of Morgan Walker—who needed help moving his slaves and his livestock south to Texas in an attempt to protect them from jayhawkers. While in Texas the war broke out. After that, it is difficult to confirm exactly what Quantrill did. It was clear enough that he tried to return to Missouri but was held up by the quickly escalating conflict. Quantrill later told Andrew Walker that when he was traveling through Indian Territory, he signed up to fight with the Cherokees under Chief Joel Mayes and fought at Wilson's Creek, where he was wounded. After receiving his wound, he returned to Jackson County. Certainly he made it back to the Walker farm sometime in the fall of that year and participated in the first neighborhood patrol in October 1861, serving under the leadership of Andrew Walker.[45]

It was not long before Quantrill became leader of the neighborhood patrol. At his father's prompting, Walker returned to his farm and left the patrol to the hired men like Jim and John Little and Quantrill. At this point, Quantrill assumed leadership and proved himself to be well suited to the role. He was daring and a good horseman and astute military commander. His daring served as something of a magnet, drawing in the young men who lived in and around Jackson County. After the neighborhood patrol attacked a group of marauding Union troopers and killed a man, Quantrill famously sent to the Union commander an affidavit that it was he and he alone who killed the Union soldier so that the Union army would not execute the Southern men they had arrested for the deed. Although he became a target for Union reprisal, Southerners believed Quantrill had made a great sacrifice, the affidavit serving as proof of his honor. Whether or not he knew it at the time, Quantrill had tapped into something in the psyche of Southern manhood, a deep-seated desire to demonstrate inner nobility through outward acts of bravery. The Southerners saw in Quantrill the best of themselves.[46]

---

45. Walker, *Recollections of Quantrill's Guerrillas*, 9–10, 13–14.

46. Ibid., 13–15, 97. The literature expounding on the significance of honor to the motivations and actions of Southern men is informative here. See Franklin, *The Militant South.* Also see Wyatt-Brown, *Southern Honor.*

Quantrill became the most dominant guerrilla leader in western Missouri. He commanded more men than any other guerrilla captain in the early years of the war. Although his personality served to draw men in, the location of his war played a major role in the size of his command. Jackson County and the surrounding counties of Clay, Lafayette, Johnson, and Cass were fertile ground for growing rebellious guerrillas. These counties were home to white farmers who were reliant upon slave labor and cash crops such as hemp and tobacco before the war. This meant that young white men, set to inherit their fathers' land and slaves, had the most to lose from the dissolution of slavery. This region was also the most affected by the troubles in Kansas and the jayhawker raids in particular, all of which pushed men to the extreme, reactionary end of the political spectrum and primed them for a war close to home. Quantrill gave these men the opportunity to realize their vengeful fantasies. Perhaps because of the sheer number of men under his command or because of his reputation as a fighter, all other guerrilla captains in the area took their lead from Quantrill. They maintained authority over their own bands, but when they were with Quantrill, they deferred to him.[47]

It is difficult to know exactly when Quantrill became recognized as *the* guerrilla chief in western Missouri. Many sources created in the postwar years seem to grant him immediate celebrity at the outset of the fighting, but this seems to be at least partially the product of hindsight. Quantrill was identified by name for the first time in the *Official Records* on February 3, 1862. Certainly, by the end of 1862 he had established himself as the overall leader of a movement so vast he could not know where it ended or who it included. Guerrilla bands that Quantrill could not possibly have known about recognized his authority. He was an icon that provided a reference point for a decentralized grassroots movement.[48]

Quantrill became fully aware of his standing in 1863. In what became the pivotal year of the war in western Missouri, Quantrill began to assert himself in new ways. For the first time he saw, understood, and tried to utilize the full potential of all the guerrillas in the region, not just the ones directly under his control. Like other transcendent commanders, Quantrill pushed beyond the traditionally recognized limits of the form

---

47. Bowen, "Guerrilla War in Western Missouri," 30–51.

48. *O.R.*, series 1, vol. 8, part 1, 57–58. For all it does in making so many primary documents accessible to historians, the *O.R.* is an imperfect collection because it is only a compendium of documents that a handful of men considered representative of the war. The documents included and those excluded were determined subjectively. Nevertheless, it can give us a general sense of when Quantrill became a known actor.

of warfare that he was waging and actively reshaped the paradigm. For instance, he first orchestrated the guerrilla movement in western Missouri so that the various bands worked in concert. Gregg remembered that "Todd, Pool, Blunt, Younger, Anderson, and others . . . each had companies and were only called together on special occasions. All of whom, however, recognized Quantrill as Commander in Chief. . . . Todd would annihilate a party of the enemy in western Jackson County. Blunt another in the eastern portion, Anderson somewhere in Kansas or Cass County, Missouri, Pool in Lafayette or Saline, Younger on the High Blue. Some one of these commanders were in collision with the enemy almost every day." Then Quantrill brought the guerrillas together into a group much larger than ten or twenty or forty. He brought a group of several hundred men together. They still broke up and scattered to gain provisions, but they did not limit the size of their band in a fight.

Quantrill used his influence to rally the guerrillas of the border around a common goal: the destruction of enemy households. After the war, Kansans and Unionists contended and historians still assert that Quantrill used his position to achieve selfish ends. For instance, Connelley suggested that Quantrill was interested only in money and that he hijacked the entire guerrilla movement just to get rich on ill-gotten plunder. Here Connelley was blinded by his disdain for Quantrill. What he could not see was something that Quantrill knew well: he was a part of a larger system of war that grew quite organically from the soil of the antebellum society of slaveholding Missouri. His role as leader of the guerrillas was functional: he was to execute the household-based warfare of the guerrillas. This meant that he owed his prominence to the community and only acted in their best interests; otherwise he would be sacked for some more desirable leader. So Quantrill's plan to unite the guerrilla bands and execute a raid on Lawrence, Kansas—that is, to take the war away from their own households, which had suffered much during the first two years of the war, and bring it into the parlors and kitchens of their enemies—was very much in keeping with the consensus attitude of the guerrillas. It took Quantrill to see the factors at work and to articulate their attitude back to the guerrillas.[49]

After the raid on Lawrence, Quantrill became infamous across the nation. In August 1863 the North was still reacting to its great victories at the battles of Gettysburg in the east and Vicksburg in the west earlier that

---

49. Connelley, *Quantrill and the Border Wars*, 309; Beilein, *Bushwhackers*, 15–45.

summer. Then, toward the end of that month, news began to trickle from the border back toward the east that the famed abolitionist outpost of Lawrence had been wiped off the map. Lawrence was a symbol of freedom and of the legitimacy of the once radical cause of abolitionism, now partly realized with the application of the Emancipation Proclamation and black men's enlistment in the Union army. Indeed, Kansas was a harbinger of many things. Not only did the fight to end slavery begin in the Kansas-Nebraska Territory, but John Brown came out of Kansas with the idea of arming slaves and turning them on their masters. Now the Union, which had once dismissed these ideas, fully adopted them. So when Quantrill struck back at their enemies' households, the North interpreted the assault on a very different level: the South was attempting to obliterate the vanguard of the Northern efforts to destroy slavery. As the leader of these dastardly Southerners, Quantrill was the worst of the worst.[50]

But Quantrill was hardly the worst. He was born in the North and never owned slaves. By all accounts, he did not kill anyone during the raid on Lawrence; in fact, he saved more people than any other guerrilla. He never participated in the mutilation that became commonplace for men like Bloody Bill Anderson, Archie Clement, George Todd, and dozens of other guerrillas. That said, Quantrill was the guerrilla chieftain during the first two years of the war, and this made him the primary recipient of criticism of the actions of men who deferred to him. His status as the worst was not a reflection of his own actions but of what men and women outside the Southern community in Missouri thought about the guerrillas.[51]

In fact, it is possible that Quantrill fell out of favor with some of his men because he was not "bad" enough. An indication of Quantrill's restraint was his decision to suspend the attack against Fort Blair at Baxter Springs. He did not have enough bloodlust to lead the bushwhackers, or

---

50. Both *Harper's Weekly* and *Frank Leslie's* ran editions with evocative pictures of the raid on Lawrence on their covers and attribute the raid to Quantrill. See "The Destruction of the City of Lawrence, Kansas and the Massacre of Its Inhabitants by the Rebel Guerrillas," *Harper's Weekly*, September 5, 1863; "The War in Kansas—Fearful Massacre at Lawrence by Quantrill's Guerrillas," *Frank Leslie's Illustrated Newspaper*, September 12, 1863.

51. Castel, who is nearly as critical of Quantrill as Connelley, actually portrays the guerrilla chieftain as reserved in terms of his personal acts of violence at Lawrence in Castel, *William Clarke Quantrill*, 122–43. Connelley's eulogy for the guerrilla chief is representative of the general Northern sentiment toward Quantrill. Connelley said, "And, so, the end came to Quantrill, the Jayhawker, the Border-Ruffian, the Bandit, the Guerrilla, the Freebooter, the Degenerate, the Depraved. . . . Of the Civil War in America he was the bloodiest man." See Connelley, *Quantrill and the Border Wars*, 482.

so Anderson, Todd, and their cronies thought. This perception was compounded during their time in Texas, where Quantrill did not participate in the revelry with many of his men. While most of the guerrillas drank and caroused, their chieftain stayed in camp, away from the saloons and brothels. Resentment welled up in both parties that manifested in a tension between Quantrill and his inner circle on one side and Anderson's band and later Todd's on the other. Eventually, Anderson and Todd seceded from Quantrill's raiders, going their own ways and leaving their old chieftain with little power or influence over the guerrilla war.[52]

For the remainder of the conflict, Quantrill was relatively insignificant in the waging of the war or in its outcome. From the time he was ostracized in spring 1864 until the late summer of that year, he retreated to a shelter in the woods of central Missouri, where he lived in relative peace with his teenage wife, Kate, while the war raged all around them. When Confederate general Sterling Price invaded the state with his army of Missourians in September 1864, the guerrillas mounted a campaign to harass the Union army in central Missouri, disrupt communication and transportation networks, and destroy any supplies they could, all in an attempt to draw attention from Price or weaken the Union force arrayed against him. Quantrill joined the effort, fighting as one of the men, not as their leader. For a few weeks, he fought side by side with some of the men he had led and took orders from guerrilla captains who had once deferred to him. When the fighting subsided, he again removed himself from the action. In 1865 Quantrill decided to go to Kentucky to carry on the fight and to link up with a formal Confederate army so that he might surrender as a soldier and receive amnesty. Before the war concluded, Quantrill and his men were ambushed. He was shot and died from his wounds in Louisville on June 6, 1865.[53]

Quantrill and the Guerrillas of Western Missouri in History

Quantrill, Gregg, and their guerrilla war have been the subjects of history books for 150 years. To properly understand the significance of the Gregg memoir in the development of this history, it is imperative to un-

---

52. Fletch Taylor letters to W. W. Scott, File 3, Box 1, Series 1, William Elsey Connelley Papers, Denver Public Library; Beilein, *Bushwhackers*, 78–110.
53. Connelley, *Quantrill and the Border Wars*, 480–83.

derstand how historians interpret the document. The way Gregg's memoir relates to histories of the war is representative of the ever-changing relationship between historians and their sources. At times this relationship was close. When it was too close, the guerrillas were not just taken at their word; historians embellished their sources' accounts in a celebration of the guerrilla cause. Other times this relationship was more distant, creating different issues, most notably an inability to see the guerrillas for who they truly were. Once the array of existing historical approaches to the Gregg memoir is surveyed and the benefits and drawbacks of each approach better understood, we can see and analyze his story from a new perspective, perhaps finding a new truth buried in an old source.[54]

The first so-called historian of the guerrilla war celebrated the guerrillas. John N. Edwards—a Confederate cavalryman turned newspaperman—set out in the postwar period to script what historian Matthew C. Hulbert calls "an irregular Lost Cause" for the border state. Edwards tried to reimagine the guerrillas as victorious in defeat. In his 1877 book, *Noted Guerrillas*, he all but omitted slavery as a cause of the war and justified the brutality of the guerrillas, who he claimed were wronged innocent men undertaking a gallant war of retribution. Quantrill was the cultural and military hero placed atop a pedestal in Edwards's pantheon of irregular Lost Cause icons. Edwards's history of the war in Missouri ran parallel to a larger effort among prominent members of the Confederate military and government to reshape the meaning of the war for posterity. These Confederate generals and politicians founded the Southern Historical Society in 1869 and used it to publish a journal that voiced the Southern perspective of the recent war. That point of view—otherwise known as the Lost Cause—claimed that Southerners did not fight for slavery but for states' rights, personal liberty, and defense of honor. Although the North was all but assured of winning due to more men and materiel, the South nevertheless fought valiantly and retained its honor. Men such as Robert E. Lee and Thomas "Stonewall" Jackson became the idols of this version of Confederate history.[55]

Quite a few Northerners saw this attempt to rewrite history for what it was—a face-saving postbellum reaction that sought to challenge the

---

54. For a lengthy discussion of the relationship between historians and bias, see Novick, *That Noble Dream.*

55. Edwards, *Noted Guerrillas*; Hulbert, "Constructing Guerrilla Memory," 58–81. For a brief summary of tone of the early Lost Cause movement for the mainstream war, see Blight, *Race and Reunion*, 79.

legitimacy of the Union victory and the social changes it brought to the South—and moved to correct the falsities of the Lost Cause narrative. The history of Quantrill's life that Edwards built up in *Noted Guerrillas* was discounted almost immediately. Edwards included in his story the lies Quantrill had told the Walkers and some of his early followers. In the 1880s, however, these lies were exposed. A man named W. W. Scott, who grew up with Quantrill in Canal Dover, began to research what had happened to his childhood acquaintance during the war. Eventually Scott traveled with Quantrill's mother, Caroline Cornelia Clarke Quantrill, to western Missouri, where they disillusioned the Southern community of the myths that Quantrill had constructed around himself. While Quantrill's mother seemed genuine and proud of her son, wishing to know the men he fought with and learn about his wartime deeds, Scott was manipulative. He saw his connection to the infamous guerrilla leader as an opportunity to achieve his own fame. Scott exploited Caroline Quantrill to gain access to her son's wartime life in a way that he was otherwise blocked from entering, all in an effort to write a book. He died before he was able to complete his biography.[56]

Even as Scott was deconstructing the Edwards's facade of the guerrillas, some of Quantrill's men used their recollections of the war to prop up the memory of their commander and their cause. Andrew Walker, Harrison Trow, and John McCorkle left accounts of their time with Quantrill. Walker told his story to a newspaperman in Texas, and it has since been published in book form. Trow's memoir offered little original material, cribbing mostly from Edwards's book and occasionally adding his own two cents. McCorkle's memoir—*Three Years with Quantrill*—is a wholly original, book-length account of the war and the author's experience in it. These men and others who wrote about fighting with Quantrill believed they possessed special insight into the man. They each believed that they knew who he was. It was their duty to stand up and testify to the truth of his character and actions. Of course, this sense of duty and fidelity also generated varying levels of bias regarding their commander's identity, the causes of the war, and the significance (or insignificance, in the guerrillas' view) of slavery and race in the war and its aftermath.[57]

56. Connelley, *Quantrill and the Border Wars*, 37–39.

57. For the memoirs that speak about fighting under Quantrill, see McCorkle, *Three Years with Quantrill*; Younger, *Confessions of a Missouri Guerrilla*; Cummings, *Jim Cummins, The Guerrilla*; Walker, *Recollections of Quantrill's Guerrillas*; Trow, *Charles W. Quantrell*.

Despite the guerrillas' written insight, Connelley came along and re-jected these guerrilla perspectives on the war out of hand. He not only worked hard to keep the essence of Gregg's memoir out of *Quantrill and the Border Wars*, but he did the same with the others, including only what fit his narrative. Walker, the definitive source of information for the events surrounding the raid on his father's farm in December 1860, told a story about Quantrill's arrival in Missouri that contradicted the story Connelley wanted to tell, so Walker was relegated to the footnotes. Connelley left out other guerrillas' accounts altogether. Perhaps it was that the Southern men of Missouri would not speak to a Kansan. Based on the way Connelley treated Gregg, however, it seemed likely that no matter how involved they were or were not in its publication, *Quantrill and the Border Wars* was always going to be a history of the guerrilla war in Missouri in which the guerrillas were mostly silent.[58]

In denying the guerrillas a voice in the history of the guerrilla war, Connelley set a precedent. His rejection of the guerrilla point of view was considered an element of scholarly objectivity. The great distance from which he wrote about the guerrilla war granted him an objective perspec-tive, which in turn validated his work. In addition to the many promises he made to Gregg, in his preface, Connelley remarked that his book was the first "serious study" of the border war and that his depiction of events on the ground would be acceptable to the Kansan. Of the Missourian, however, he said, "The time has not yet come when a dispassionate study of the conditions which existed in Missouri will be acceptable to all the people of that great commonwealth." In other words, *Quantrill and the Borders Wars* was "a dispassionate study," but some of the people who read it—namely Missourians—might not be so detached, a clever deflection in which Connelley flipped any concerns of bias from himself onto the reader.[59]

The first professional historian to write about the guerrillas followed some of Connelley's approach. Historian Richard S. Brownlee begins his book *Gray Ghosts of the Confederacy: Guerrilla Warfare in the West, 1861–1865* (1958) by stating, "This book is based on historical facts." Claiming that his history is based on just the facts is to make the same assertion as his predecessors, that he looked at his subject through an objective lens.

---

58. For an idea of how Connelley used the evidence from Walker, see Connelley, *Quan-trill and the Border Wars*, 154n5, 159–60n6.

59. Connelley, *Quantrill and the Border Wars*, 5–6.

That said, Brownlee does not assert the omniscient perspective his fellow historians do. To his credit, he tells his readers that other historians "in writing of the time, have chosen to present the events [in Missouri's guerrilla war] as inevitable," but "it is the opinion of the author, after years of research and study, that the men dealt with here, in common with men of all other ages, were men of free will." For Brownlee, this means that "there seems to be no reason to withhold from them praise or condemnation they deserve as they created history." He humanizes his subject and in doing so humanizes himself.[60]

Brownlee's straightforward approach carries over to his use of sources, such as the Gregg memoir. He cites Gregg throughout his book but refuses to become dependent on him. Nor does Brownlee reject the perspective of the guerrilla, knowing that men like Gregg were the only ones who had insight on a great deal of the guerrilla war. In fact, he does not feel the need to judge Gregg or his memoir one way or another in an explicit way, letting his history speak for itself. Rather than bludgeon readers with his conclusions, Brownlee comes across as confident, above the fray. He seems to trust in his readers' intelligence.[61]

With the possible exception of Brownlee's work, the themes of *distance* and *objectivity* Connelley established recur in several significant academic histories written about the guerrilla war in Missouri. At the centennial of the Civil War, Albert Castel became the first professional scholar to write a biography of Quantrill. On the whole, Castel's book *William Clarke Quantrill: His Life and Times* (1962) is a good example of professional scholarship and has persisted through the years as *the* credible scholarly biography of the guerrilla chieftain in no small part because of Castel's meticulous research. Nevertheless, Castel appears to follow Connelley's example in at least one way. Looking back on the original publication of *William Clarke Quantrill*, Castel writes in his 1999 edition of the book that he "undertook to write a biography of [Quantrill] that would strike a balance between Edwards and Connelley. . . . I was able to remain objective and avoid partisan writing, unlike Edwards, who was an ex-Confederate officer, and Connelley, whose ancestors fought in the Civil War (mine did not)." Yet entire chapters of Castel's book are summaries of some of the most obviously biased parts of *Quantrill and the Border Wars* that he chose to include even after noting his predecessor's extreme bias. Although

---

60. Brownlee, *Gray Ghosts of the Confederacy*, vii–viii.
61. Brownlee, *Gray Ghosts of the Confederacy*.

borrowing directly from Connelley, he completely avoids including any part of Edwards's narrative. Castel's biography of Quantrill is still cited by anyone working on the guerrilla war in Missouri, allowing Connelley's narrative to seep into modern studies.[62]

This is not to criticize the substance of Castel's historical work on the guerrillas. It is well within the standards of the historical profession to choose which sources to include and which sources to omit. Indeed, it is imperative to the evolution of historical study that the historian bring to bear her or his best evidence in making the case. Presuming historians are not including clearly fraudulent sources, misrepresenting their sources, plagiarizing, fabricating, or otherwise intending to deceive their audiences, they must use the materials at their disposal in a way that helps them to offer a new perspective on past events.[63]

However, the claims of objectivity in the study of the guerrilla war are problematic. In the 1999 edition of *William Clarke Quantrill*, Castel acknowledges the challenge that lays at the heart of these claims. After claiming his own ability to be objective, Castel writes, "I am a professionally trained historian who believes that in writing history one should strive to achieve the maximum degree of accuracy and objectivity even though you know that, being human, you will inevitably make errors of fact and judgement." Such a noble sentiment is deserving of praise. But this statement, or some version of it, has been uttered, written, and printed time and again, and every time it taints what follows because objectivity is not only impossible, but the use of the term is deceptive. Whether it is intentional or subconscious, a promise of objectivity works to cloak subjectivity; it obscures more than it reveals.[64]

In recent decades the perceived distance between historians and the guerrillas of Civil War Missouri has increased, and with it the claims of objectivity have intensified. The best encapsulation of this sentiment comes from Michael Fellman, who, in the introduction to his watershed work *Inside War: The Guerrilla Conflict in Missouri during the American Civil War*, writes, "I seek to describe, without romanticizing them but also without degrading or dismissing them, ordinary nineteenth-century Americans going through terrible times." Fellman acknowledges that despite

---

62. Castel, *William Clarke Quantrill*, 22–45, 23fn; Castel, *William Clarke Quantrill* (1999), x.

63. The American Historical Association has outlined the basic standards of the profession of history in American Historical Association, *Statement on Standards of Professional Conduct* (Washington, D.C.: American Historical Association, 2011).

64. Castel, *William Clarke Quantrill* (1999), x.

his best intentions to remain neutral in studying the guerrilla war, there is a certain hazard that swirls about writing a history of such bloody and contentious warfare. He writes, "Becoming contemptuous is a danger for peaceful academics deploying their cool medium to discuss violence." In a lifetime of powerful analysis, this is perhaps Fellman's most incisive observation.[65]

Fellman attempts to rise above this peril in his study of Civil War Missouri. In so doing, he elevates his historical perspective of the war to something like that of a bird's-eye view of the guerrilla war, which gives his work a great breadth of vision. From that vantage point, Fellman constructs a mosaic of human experiences, seemingly endless snapshots of violence that when plastered together allow him to conjure up significant conclusions about the interior of war. Fellman's argument in *Inside War* reflects a broad view of this multicolored, kaleidoscopic miscellany of bloody acts taking place across the state. He quite persuasively contends that the guerrilla conflict was society boiled down into nihilistic chaos without beginning, middle, or end.[66]

By looking at the war in Missouri writ large rather than just at Quantrill or his band, Fellman's research included massive collections of sources like the Provost Marshals' Files Relating to Individual Citizens, other records generated by Union officers who served in Missouri, and letters and diaries of women and others typically imagined outside the boundaries of warfare. In including such sources, he broke a path for future scholarship on the war. After processing cart after cart of boxes full of documents, Fellman selected an array of evidence from across the war to construct his topically organized work, treating nearly all sources the same. Whether it was the report of Union officers fighting the guerrillas, official correspondence from Confederate officials, Union military policies, or letters from so-called civilians, he read documents for their significance, extracting evidence as he went.[67]

The exception was Fellman's use of the Gregg memoir and other guerrilla-produced source material, about which he appears conflicted. Throughout most of *Inside War*, the words of the guerrillas are given little play. However, in the final chapter, "After the War," he grapples more directly with the works of Gregg and other guerrillas, offering a close read of these sources and their significance in the context of the postwar pe-

---

65. Fellman, *Inside War*, xx.
66. Fellman, *Inside War*, xvi.
67. Fellman, *Inside War*, xvi.

riod. Fellman concludes that the guerrillas "expended much energy after the war in justifying their wartime activities to others and themselves" and that they mostly fabricated their stories about the war to cope with their wartime deeds—a way of easing their consciences—and to sway public opinion. In raising questions about the guerrillas' motivations and the overall significance of guerrilla memory in manipulating the popular image of the Southern guerrilla, Fellman's work goes a long way toward dismantling the most harmful elements of the Lost Cause.[68]

Fellman's focus on the Gregg memoir reveals tensions between a historian writing from outside the war from a great distance and a man who lived within the war and attempted to write an unbiased perspective. Despite the fact that Connelley—a radical in his own right—concluded that Gregg was perhaps the only reliable source for the guerrilla war, Fellman cites Gregg as wholly unreliable for his "reworking of memory." He analyzes the Gregg memoir in some depth, mentioning Gregg and his memoir more than half a dozen times in just a few pages.[69] In Fellman's hands, the Gregg memoir appears threatening, the work of a liar and a propagandist for the Confederacy.[70]

Rather than resolving the tension between the guerrilla's perspective and the historian's, Fellman's treatment of the Gregg memoir stretches the distance between these two viewpoints to an uncomfortable degree. Compounding the problem is his misquoting of the Gregg memoir at a pivotal point in his analysis. According to Fellman, "William Gregg claimed that one day he had been standing by while Union men burned Mrs. Crawford's house. When two of the Union men had 'snatched a lace cap from [her] head and threw it into the flames of the burning building,' Gregg disregarded all danger, whipped out his pistols, and killed both men." Although this sounds like something Fellman's guerrillas might have said, Gregg did not say it in his memoir. There was an instance of the Crawford home being burned and Crawford's cap being ripped from her head on that cold winter day; the rest of the story, however, cannot be located in any documents that relate to Gregg.[71]

However this misquotation made its way into Fellman's book, mistakes happen in history just as they do in the lives of the people historians seek to study, or as Castel wisely said, "being human, you will inevitably

68. Fellman, *Inside War*, 247, 247–63.

69. See pages 253–56.

70. Fellman, *Inside War*, 254.

71. Fellman, *Inside War*, 255–56, 307n36.

make errors of fact and judgement." Fellman was right about one thing: perilous, indeed, is the writing and reading of guerrilla history. If historians get too close, as Edwards did, they risk falling under the spell of the bushwhackers and becoming their mouthpiece. If historians create too much distance between their subject matter and themselves, they may never be able to truly see the guerrillas, let alone understand them. Pitfalls abound.[72]

In reading the Gregg memoir, beware but be not timid. In reading his or any other histories of the guerrilla war, reject claims of objectivity, and be on guard whenever an author makes such assertions. Instead, the reader must embrace humanity—his own, Gregg's, that of the men Gregg and his cohort killed, and that of the historians (including the one who writes these words) who have tried to re-create the guerrilla war on the page. Although Castel and Fellman highlight the flaws of humanity in their approaches to historical study, remember that within our shared humanity lives the greatest tool of the historian: empathy. The Gregg memoir offers a rare opportunity to enter the world of Civil War Missouri. Put down your preconceptions and brace for a hellish and invigorating ride across a strange landscape.

---

72. Ibid. Fellman's mistakes are relatively minor in comparison to some of the major academic controversies. See Hoffer, *Past Imperfect*; Castel, *William Clarke Quantrill* (1999), x.

Editorial Method

THE MEMOIR WAS TRANSCRIBED FROM the copy of the handwritten original at the State Historical Society of Missouri (which has absorbed the holdings of the University of Missouri's Western Historical Manuscript Collection). I gathered William H. Gregg's correspondence with William E. Connelley, the contracts laying out the original ownership of Gregg's memoir, and three shorter recollections from Gregg from the McCain Library and Archives at the University of Southern Mississippi, Spencer Research Library at the University of Kansas, and the Denver Public Library. The Gregg-Connelley correspondence is gathered together in a stand-alone section of this volume, and the other stories and the contracts appear in the four addenda.

Regarding the annotation and editing of the memoir and his correspondence, I have worked to preserve Gregg's voice and elucidate his story. The memoir, which was always intended for publication, has been edited to correct grammar, spelling, and punctuation mistakes to meet modern standards. Quite a few phrases and sentences were written in antiquated or awkward ways but were still composed within the bounds of proper grammar, so I have chosen to leave them as is to preserve Gregg's particular style. Where sentences were fragmented or convoluted, punctuation has been added, subtracted, or altered to promote clarity.

I have chosen to handle Gregg's correspondence differently because he never thought it would be published or even read by anyone other than Connelley. Rather than edit it down into a publishable form and style, I have let Gregg's words, sentences, and paragraphs remain mostly as they were written to give readers a better sense of how the ex-guerrilla expressed himself in a more casual and intimate context. I have annotated both the memoir and his correspondence to illuminate the finer points of Gregg's history.

A Little Dab of
History without
Embellishment

————————

By William H. Gregg

History after history has been written of Quantrill and his men, none of which can be characterized as true. And that which is not true is not history. About the twenty-fifth day of December 1861, James A. Hendricks, John W. Koger, and I joined Quantrill's command, then consisting, all told, of eight men, we three swelling his force to eleven. We found Quantrill at Mrs. Samuel Crumps's place, on Independence and Blue Springs Road, and this was the nucleus to the greatest guerrilla band the world ever produced. Quantrill at that time was about twenty-four years of age. He had blue-gray eyes, red beard, and hair so light that many of the boys denominated him "tow head," but as the years rolled on his hair acquired a more sandy cast.[1]

Quantrill (his story to the contrary notwithstanding) was born at Canal Dover, Ohio; at least a woman said to be his mother says he was born there. Quantrill told me this story: "Me and my older brother, with a wagon and team and a negro boy, started for Pike's Peak. Arriving at Lawrence, we stopped to make some purchases, leaving sometime in the afternoon, and camped near the Kaw River, where we were attacked by Montgomery's jayhawkers. My brother was killed, I was wounded and left for dead, and the negro, wagon, and team appropriated. After keeping vigil for twenty-four hours amidst the hideous howling of hundreds of coyotes, I was becoming almost famished for water. I managed to crawl to the river and quench my thirst, after which I espied a canoe at the opposite bank. Soon after, an Indian approached the canoe to whom I hollered, asking him to come over, which he did. After hearing my story, he buried my dead brother and took me to his cabin, where he

---

1. John Koger was twenty-six years old in 1861, with a young wife and two small children. He was a neighbor of the Greggs. Hendricks was twenty-eight when the war began. He was a merchant from Kentucky living in the same neighborhood as Gregg and Koger. 1860 U.S. Federal Manuscript Census, Jackson County, Mo. Albert Castel says that the original members of the band "were Bill Haller, Jim and John Little, Ed and John Koger, Harrison Trace, Joe Gilchrist, Bill Gregg, Joe Vaughn, and George Todd." He does not mention Hendricks, and he misidentifies Harrison Trow as Harrison Trace. See Castel, *William Clarke Quantrill*, 66.

and his wife nursed me to health. After that I took myself to Lawrence and joined Montgomery's band under the name of Charley Hart. I soon found I had the confidence of Montgomery, his officers, and men. I next obtained the names of all the men who had taken part in the killing of my brother, etc. I at once went to work in a systematic way to get revenge for the wrongs heaped upon me and my brother. I managed to get one at a time away from the command and never permitted one to get back alive, until, when the war came on, only two were left."[2]

The above story, however, was somewhat shaken when a woman purporting to be Quantrill's mother and a Mr. Scott—both from Canal Dover, Ohio—told me that Quantrill had no older brother. Scott asserted that he and William Clarke Quantrill were schoolboys together and that he could not account for Quantrill's taking the stand he did in the war, "for," said Scott, "he was raised an abolitionist." Whether Quantrill was a deception thus far or not rests with the truth or falsity of the latter statement. One thing I do know, however, and that is that he was a soldier and not afraid to die and that he was equitable and just to friend and foe up to a certain period in the war, a matter that I will treat more fully hereafter.

Quantrill and his men have been unjustly slandered by the people of the North, a people who even to this day know nothing of them except what they have read in irresponsible books and newspapers. The time has come when their minds should be disabused. Quantrill's command was composed principally of men and boys from the very best families of Missouri, and now at this writing many of them are honored citizens of Missouri and other states. Many have been honored with high political positions, not in Missouri alone but other states also, and none of them have ever defaulted a record of which I am exceptionally proud. You must not infer that I make this claim for all men who chanced to be with Quantrill. It would be a miracle if such was the case. It was the Kansan who hated and berated Quantrill and his men more zealously than any other people, but if Quantrill and his men were the very greatest demons and sprang from the very depths of degradation, they could not have been any worse than the Kansan. For the Kansan to berate them I would liken to the pot calling the kettle black.

Quantrill and his men had many ups and downs. They were often in the greatest of peril, foot sore, hungry and shot at from every quarter,

2. Connelley, *Quantrill and the Border Wars*, 17–173; Castel, *William Clarke Quantrill*, 22–45; McCorkle, *Three Years with Quantrill*, 53–57, 218n2.

hunted day in and day out, staying in the enemy's country where they were outnumbered two hundred to five hundred to one. And yet none of them were known to murmur at their hard lot.[3]

Outside the Kansas City *Star*, the Kansan is our most bitter enemy. The great fault in the people who write of us is that they only tell one side of the story, just as though they had the right to murder, burn, rob, and steal, and those whom they murdered, robbed, and plundered had no right to resist. General Sherman very truly said that war was *hell* and meant to kill, and that is what the Kansan did when he came to Missouri and their killing was principally of old men and boys, noncombatants. I will have more to say of the sainted Kansan in the other chapter.

Quantrill and his men did little more than stand the enemy off after I joined the command until spring, during which time we captured many of the enemy whom we universally paroled. Quantrill and his men were vying with each other over who should be the most magnanimous toward prisoners up to March 20, 1862, when we received Major General Halleck's order telling his officers and men to shoot or hang Quantrill or his men wherever caught or found. At this date we had sixty men, twenty of whom had come to us only the day before, and when the order was read and explained to them, these recent recruits left us. They were disgusted at the idea of being outlawed and the hoisting of the black flag by the enemy. They did not stay away long, however, as the Federal troops began murdering by wholesale—old men and boys—and were so insulting to the women that they too often hid out on their approach. Heaven bless the women. They were friends in need, and, indeed, no braver and truer women lived than the Southern ladies of Missouri. We often owed our lives to them. So I say again, heaven bless them.[4]

On February 22, 1862, it being George Washington's birthday, Quantrill with fifteen men went to Independence, not knowing the enemy

---

3. For more about the guerrillas being hunted, see Beilein, *Bushwhackers*, 214–42.

4. *O.R.*, series 1, vol. 8, 463–64. Gregg is not alone in his praise for the "ladies." A number of other guerrillas proclaim their thanks for the women who assisted them in the war effort. Hamp "Babe" Watts offers a very telling observation about the relationship between the guerrillas and their women. According to Watts, "These young men loved women and the women loved them." See Watts, *Babe of the Company*, 12. For more discussion of the role played by women in Missouri's Civil War, see Whites, *Gender Matters*; Whites, "'Corresponding with the Enemy': Mobilizing the Relational Field of Battle in St. Louis," in *Occupied Women: Gender, Military Occupation, and the American Civil War*, ed. LeeAnn Whites and Alecia P. Long (Baton Rouge: Louisiana State University Press, 2009), 103–16; Whites, "Forty Shirts," 56–78.

was there. On our arrival we were met by an Ohio cavalry regiment. Of course there was a collision, and while we lost two men and the enemy held the town, we had the better of the fight, their losses being much greater than ours. Toward the close of the engagement, a sturdy, brave Ohio cavalryman rode up beside me with drawn saber. Thinking that I was a comrade, he soon found his mistake and proceeded to belabor me with his saber. The only harm he did was to blacken my arm from the elbow to the wrist.[5]

Soon after this, on March 22, Quantrill with twenty-one men were surrounded at what was known as the Tate house, fourteen miles south of Kansas City. After fighting the enemy for an hour, they fired the house. Quantrill and his men made a dash, drove the enemy back, and escaped with the loss of their horses and one man Perry Hoy, captured, of whom I will speak of more fully hereafter.[6]

While it is a notorious fact that we were, as a rule, greatly outnumbered by the enemy, they always gave way to our charge. From this date to about the middle of April, it was a series of surprises for Quantrill and his men, in each case losing our horses, which was a great drawback. However, we soon got on to the enemy's tactics and never afterwards did we lose horses in any considerable number but often beat the enemy out of theirs.

About April 10, 1862, Quantrill with twenty men camped at a vacant house known as the Lowe house, sixteen miles southeast of Kansas City, where he was betrayed by some unknown person. Having no guard out, he was surrounded at dawn next morning by Lieutenant Nash, with about sixty men. The first thing Nash did was to secure the horses. Next, he surrounded the house and demanded a surrender, which of course was refused. The men were sound asleep and of course when wakened by the fire from the enemy were addled and confused. However, the men, except Andrew Blunt and Joe Gilchrist, fought their way out and escaped. The two mentioned were captured, taken out, and set upon a stump for a target. Gilchrist was killed; Blunt's arm was broken. Nash, coming up

---

5. There is no description of the skirmish at Independence, Mo., on this date in the *O.R.* other than that it occurred, as is stated in the "Summary of Principle Events," *O.R.*, series 1, vol. 8, 2.

6. John McCorkle offered a version of the Tate house ambush that corroborates Gregg's recollection. See McCorkle, *Three Years with Quantrill*, 68–72. For information on Perry Hoy, see Brownlee, *Gray Ghosts of the Confederacy*, 58, 101. Hoy was one of the early members of Quantrill's band. Castel, *William Clarke Quantrill*, 66, 95–96.

at this juncture, stopped the shooting and saved Blunt, who was taken to Independence and placed in the hospital, from which he escaped through the connivance of Dr. Port, who was forced to act as surgeon for the troops stationed there. This misfortune left one-half our men without horses.[7]

The second day after the Lowe house affair, Tucker, Gregg, and Estes were encamped near Stony Point where John Keshlear came to them. Dr. Herndon was at the house of Jacob Gregg, and James Tucker, desiring to see the doctor, rode to the house and called him to the fence. While talking to the doctor, a scout of seventy-five federals came within fifty yards before they were discovered. Tucker's horse became unmanageable and threw him. Before he could rise to his feet, the enemy were in fifteen feet of him with presented guns. Nothing daunted, Tucker rose, drew his revolver, presenting it at the enemy, and walked backward until he reached the brush. Then he wheeled and ran and escaped without a scratch. Keshlear, although he had been warned not to leave the camp, had started for the house on foot. Being a cripple he could not run fast and was overhauled and killed. Tucker, Estes, and Gregg escaped but lost their horses.[8]

A few days later, however, Tucker was captured at Pink Hill by a company of Germans, which held Tucker prisoner. About the third night of Tucker's captivity, he played a ruse on his guard and escaped. Quantrill at this time was camped at the house of Samuel Clark, three miles south of Stony Point. Tucker came to us on Saturday evening. The next morning Gregg was acting barber, cutting a comrade's hair in the front yard. John Koger had ridden out to the house of an acquaintance, returned, and dismounted in front of the house, where he was hitching his horse. Suddenly Koger made a move that showed he had sighted the enemy. Immediately after Koger had shown this sign, which would be utterly impossible for me to describe, the enemy fired upon him. One of their bullets

---

7. According to Union sources, Lieutenant Nash had thirty men with him, and they killed four guerrillas and wounded four others. See *O.R.*, series 1, vol. 13, 58.

8. William Tucker was a twenty-nine-year-old head of household and farm owner with a wife and a small family in Jackson County when the war began. Estes was likely one of two brothers—Daniel or Alvis Estes—who were twenty-one and nineteen when the war began and lived in their parents' household in Sni-A-Bar Township, Jackson County. John Keshlear was twenty-one years old at the outset of the war. Before the war, he had worked his family's Jackson County farm for his widowed mother. 1860 U.S. Federal Manuscript Census, Jackson County, Mo.

struck a rail in fence, glanced, and struck Koger on the buttock, burning him severely but not breaking the skin. I imagine I can see Koger holding the burnt spot now.[9]

After an hour's fighting from the house (which was log), we divided the men, leaving Todd in charge at the house. Quantrill and Gregg went to the barn to secure the horses, but before we had accomplished anything, Todd became alarmed and yelled for us to come to his aid, for which there was no possible excuse. On the return of Quantrill and Gregg with their force to the house, it was decided to abandon the house and our horses. I contended then and have always contended that if Todd had done his whole duty we would have saved our horses. After leaving the house, we made a detour through the timber, reaching the crossing on the Sni ahead of the forces we had fought at Clark's, just in time, however, to meet reinforcements coming to their aid from Pink Hill. We lay concealed behind rocks, trees, et cetera, allowed the enemy to ride into the stream, and opened fire, wounding several. At this juncture, the force we had fought at Clark's came upon our rear, and we drove it away. The slight wound received by Koger at Clark's was the only damage received by us.[10]

Quantrill and his men being dismounted, without a sufficient supply of ammunition, especially caps, Quantrill and Todd went to Hannibal, Missouri, where they sold their horses and bought caps, returning (via railroad) by way of Saint Joseph and Platte City. At the latter place, they hired a hack for Kansas City. Arriving at or near Harlem, Clay County, opposite of Kansas City, sometime in the night, the hackman was hailed by a picket. Quantrill and Todd slipped out of the hack and escaped without being seen, either by the hackman or the enemy. Going down the river, the next day they came upon Blunt and Bledsoe fishing from a skiff on the Missouri River. The meeting was a surprise for both parties, for when Quantrill left for Hannibal, Blunt was in the hand of the enemy, and neither Blunt nor Bledsoe knew of Quantrill's trip. Crossing over to Jackson County, Quantrill found most of his men had procured horses and were fairly well mounted. Collecting ten or twelve men, he at once went about

---

9. Samuel Clark was a Virginia-born farmer who was fifty-five at the outset of the war. He had little family living with him, only a twenty-one-year-old woman, in 1860. 1860 U.S. Federal Manuscript Census, Jackson County, Mo.

10. "The Sni" was the Sni-A-Bar Creek that meandered through Jackson and Lafayette Counties with low bottomland on both banks that was covered in thick brush. The Sni-A-Bar region had been home to quite a few guerrillas before the war. This fact, coupled with the geography, made for a perfect guerrilla haunt.

reassuring his men and sympathizers by devising an ambuscade at what was called Blue Cut, six miles south of Independence. There he almost annihilated a troop of the enemy who were escorting the mail to Harrisonville.

After the first of May of this year, recruiting officers flocked to Jackson and adjoining counties. Among them was Colonel Upton Hayes, and there was no more brave or dauntless spirit falling in with Quantrill. Arriving on Walnut Creek in the northwest corner of Henry County, we camped at a vacant farm house, threw out pickets, and rested for the night. Soon after breakfast the next morning, our pickets were driven in by a scout of ninety-six men. We, having exactly the same number, fought and drove them away. One of their wounded fell into our hands, who (notwithstanding they had hoisted the black flag against us) we tenderly carried to the house of a citizen. Hayes, having come up from the south on July 10 for the purpose of recruiting a regiment, was restless. He asked Quantrill for an escort to Jackson. Quantrill gave him Todd with thirty men, reducing our force to sixty-five men.[11]

Of course the fight in the morning had stirred up a hornets nest, and about three o'clock p.m. the enemy came after us three or four hundred strong. We very gracefully retired, leaving the field to the enemy. Encountering a severe rain storm, which soaked us to the hide, we soon left the enemy in the distance, stopping to feed where Strasburg now stands, some eight miles east of Pleasant Hill. But on approach of night we resumed our march. Passing a half-mile south of Pleasant Hill, garrisoned with several hundred troops, we recrossed Big Creek. Coming to a thickly wooded locality four or five miles west of the town, we lay down and slept till morning, when we moved to the house of one Searaucy, camping in the horse lot.[12]

The morning was bright and lovely; the many wild birds were caroling in the woods. Our boys were jubilant, Hicks George and Bob Houk were sent on our back trail as pickets. Blankets, overcoats, et cetera hung upon the lot fence to dry for about two hours after our stop. Firing at our picket line warned us of the approach of the enemy. Blankets and cloth-

---

11. For information on Upton Hayes, see Brownlee, *Gray Ghosts of the Confederacy*, 79, 91–92, 100–101. Hayes and seven other colonels were sent to Missouri by Confederate general Thomas C. Hindman to commission guerrilla officers and recruit units to fight for the Confederacy during the summer of 1862. Castel, *William Clarke Quantrill*, 81.

12. The only people named Searcy who lived in the area were living north of the spot that Gregg described. It is unclear whose farm this was.

ing were snatched from the fence and our horses saddled and hitched. In a steep gulch in the rear, men were ordered to the front, where they lay low concealed from the approaching enemy with instructions not to fire until ordered. It was only seconds after the pickets got in until here come at a dead run six men commanded by a sergeant. At this time I was midway in the lot, the only man the enemy could see, and of course drew their fire. The men lay in silence behind the lot fence. Quantrill stood behind the gate post with hand on the latch, owning to the fact that I was the only man the enemy could see. It seemed to me an hour for the bullets were whizzing thick and fast around me.[13]

Finally, when the enemy were in forty to sixty feet, the order was given. The men fired; the seven federals fell in a heap, their horses coming straight toward the gate. I yelled to Quantrill to open the gate, which he did, the horses coming into the lot. On approaching the seven dead federals, we found seven six-round Colt carbines, seven Colt navies, and seven bottles or canteens of whiskey, all of which we appropriated. In a few moments the main body of the enemy came up, two hundred strong, and formed one hundred yards away, where we fought them for some moments. Being armed with guns of longer range than ours, their fire was telling on us. We had one man killed (John Hampton) and two wounded (Geo. Mattox and Wm. Tucker). Tucker being able to travel, we sent him away in his brother's charge. When this damage had been done, we climbed the fence and charged them on foot, driving them away.

They retired to a farm house on the prairie in plain view of us, where we could see the surgeons dressing wounds. Throwing a picket out to watch this force, we set about to remove our dead and wounded. The farmer having no horse wagon, we found a yoke of cattle, which we hitched to the wagon. Placing rails on the wagon, with two feather beds on the rails, we put the dead Hampton on the beds and the wounded man, Mattox, who was shot through the lungs, beside him. All this time a cloud was gathering. The enemy, already two hundred strong, had been reinforced, with the reinforcements being concealed from us. When we were ready to move, the enemy in sight began to move on us, and at this juncture a laughable incident occurred. Dave Pool with another man was placed in a pasture to watch the enemy, in which there was a huge jack. About the same time the enemy moved on our picket, the jack spied the

---

13. Hicks George had a brother named Hiram "Hi" George. Hi was the grandfather of the amateur historian who was the last private owner of the handwritten Gregg memoir. It was donated from his estate to the State Historical Society of Missouri.

picket also and made a dash for them at a dead run with his tail hoisted straight in the air, his immense ears laid back, braying at every jump. Pool said afterwards that he was in double fear and did not know by which he would be run down, the federals or the jack.[14]

We had not gone more than three-eighths of a mile until the enemy was on us, forcing us to give up our dead and wounded and forcing us to dismount. Here was enacted the greatest, most unequal battle scene that I ever witnessed—the enemy being 450 strong and our force being 61 rank and file. We were surrounded in less than a moment. We received a galling fire from all sides. The nature of the ground chosen by us was such that the enemy was forced to relinquish its hold on the east and west. We never divided our men but fought a side at a time, making great havoc in the Federal ranks. The troops we were fighting were well-trained, brave soldiers, but unfortunately for them, they were loaded up with whiskey and continually rushed upon us, the very thing we wanted them to do for our men were armed with pistols and shot guns and could do but little execution at long range.

After the fight had continued for two hours, without the loss of a man killed and only one wounded (that one being Quantrill), many of the men became short of ammunition. On inquiry, it was found that Pool, in his flight from the jack and the enemy, had lost our extra supply. Quantrill then ordered the men to mount and get out, but before they could retire they had to beat the enemy back with rocks, which were very plentiful about the ground over which we fought. After all the men who could get their horses were mounted, Ezra Moore was shot from his horse and killed, the first man to fall in the fight. Jerre Doors, in trying to get his horse, was shot through the knee and died from the wound. Our wounded all fell into the hands of the enemy—the only time our wounded were treated with anything like courtesy by the Federal government. They also captured one man, who was unhurt, and exchanged him—the only one of our men ever exchanged by the Federal government.[15]

For a month after this wonderful fight, there was a lull. Quantrill hid away nursing his wound, which was only partially healed when we fought

---

14. The "jack" Gregg is referring to is a jackass, or a mule.

15. According to the census, Ezra Moore was twenty-four years old in 1860 and was married to the nineteen-year-old Frances Moore. They had no children. He was born in Ohio, and his wife was born in Missouri. He likely worked for Mary Hudson, a fifty-one-year-old widow with a large farm whose household was adjacent to Moore's place. 1860 Federal Manuscript Census, Jackson County, Mo., 186.

at Independence on the eleventh day of August 1862, in which Quantrill
with twenty-five men took an active part. In my judgment, the fight would
have been lost only for Quantrill and his men. We guided the little army
to the town, cut Buel off from his men, and closed the battle by forcing
the surrender of Buel and his bodyguard, who were barricaded in the
McCoy Bank Building. Quantrill lost one man killed in this battle, Kit
Chiles.[16]

The little army that captured Independence was composed principally
of Col. Upton Hayes's regiment, but few of whom had been in battle. Col.
J. T. Hughes with about seventy-five men and Quantrill with twenty-five
men were the only veterans in the fight, but they all stood the test just
the same. Two or three days after the taking of Independence, Quantrill
and his men were sworn into the Confederate service and reorganized by
electing Quantrill captain, William Haller first lieutenant, George Todd
second lieutenant, and William H. Gregg third lieutenant, with 150 men.
The next day after we were sworn in, Quantrill with ninety men repaired
to Independence to secure commissaries captured and left there. Lieutenants Haller and Gregg were left with sixty men six miles west from
Lone Jack with orders not to move without orders from him unless we
should be driven away. Cockrell, having come in from the South and
joined forces with Hayes, was encamped near Lone Jack.[17]

Major Foster, a brave and energetic Federal officer with eight hundred
men, came to Lone Jack in search of these Confederate forces. About
eight o'clock on the morning of the sixteenth of August, a courier from
Colonel Hayes arrived at our camp with a dispatch asking us to come to
their assistance. Haller refused to go until a second courier came. He was
persuaded by Gregg to go, although it was a disobedience of orders. Although the distance was covered in short order, we were too late to take
part in the fight, though we captured about 150 prisoners. It was here
that Cole Younger displayed the greatest of magnanimity in that he saved
the life of Major Foster and his brother and also saved them some seven
or eight hundred dollars in money.[18]

The time has come that I must speak of Perry Hoy again and tell of
scenes that were repugnant to me. At the Battle of Lone Jack a Lieu-

---

16. Gerteis, *The Civil War in Missouri*, 145–46.
17. Ibid.; Cockrell was Jeremiah Vardaman Cockrell, who fought for the South in the
Missouri State Guard and the Confederate army. See Brownlee, *Gray Ghosts of the Confederacy*, 92–93.
18. Gerteis, *The Civil War in Missouri*, 146–47.

tenant Copland was captured, a man who was very obnoxious to the Southern soldier and citizen—a man who had, in cold blood, murdered numerous old men, among them two of the Longacres of Johnson County. When Colonel Upton Hayes was ready to leave for the South, he turned Lieutenant Copland over to Quantrill. We had established a camp some four miles northeast of the now town of Lee's Summit. Late one evening, Charles Cowherd and William Howard came to our camp bringing with them a copy of the then Missouri *Republican*, in which was published an account of the shooting of Perry Hoy, our man captured at the Tate house on the twenty-second of March. Quantrill was sitting at a table reading the paper, and I was sitting by waiting to see the paper when suddenly I saw a change in Quantrill's countenance, and the paper fell from his hand. Without saying a word he drew a blank book from his pocket, penned a note on a leaf, and folded and handed it to me, saying, "give this to Blount." He then told me that Hoy had been shot. Eager to see the purport of the note, I opened and read, "take Lieut. Copland out and shoot him, go to Woodsmall's camp, get two prisoners and shoot them." On the return of Blount, the men were ordered to saddle up and on inquiry found that we were going to Kansas to kill ten men in revenge for poor Hoy.

Let's have the full sequel to this killing: Hoy was captured on the night of the twenty-second of March at the Tate house. Soon after the capture of Hoy, we captured a first lieutenant of a Kansas cavalry regiment, whom we held to exchange for Hoy. Quantrill wrote the commanding officer at Fort Leavenworth asking that the exchange be made but got no answer. He then sent the lieutenant to Leavenworth to effect an exchange. On the return of the lieutenant, he told Quantrill that they refused to make the exchange and asked Quantrill what he was going to do with him. Quantrill told him to go home. The lieutenant remarked that he would go home and stay there, that he would not fight for a government that would not exchange a private for him, a lieutenant.

After the shooting of the prisoners north of Lee's Summit, we marched in the neighborhood of Red Bridge near the Kansas line, remaining there until the next evening, when we marched on Olathe. We had killed ten men before we reached Olathe, but we had started to take Olathe. Arriving near the place, Quantrill ordered Lieutenant Gregg to advance with sixty men and place a cordon around the town so that no one might escape while Quantrill with the remainder of the command marched to the center of the town. On the arrival of Quantrill at the court square, he found 125 soldiers drawn up on the sidewalk south of the square, so a plan was adopted to capture these men without bloodshed. The men were ordered to hitch their horses to the courtyard fence, close together, and when hitched to step to the rear of their horses, standing in line. This completed, they drew their revolvers and ordered the federals to surrender, which they did without firing a shot. However, one man refused to give up his gun and was shot and killed. So we had killed fourteen men for Hoy.

We remained in Olathe until morning, when we marched our prisoners out on the prairie about two miles from town, swore them out of the service, and turned them loose—notwithstanding Major General Halleck's order to shoot or hang Quantrill and his men wherever caught or found. About two weeks after the capture of Olathe, Colonel Burris with his Kansas regiment came upon us near Columbus, in Johnson County, Missouri. His force being so much greater than ours, we retreated to Lafayette County, avoiding a collision. While encamped at the farm of one Harvey Gleaves, some of our pickets were chased in and came near being captured. At first we thought it was Burris's command following us up but soon found they were militia from Lexington. We gave pursuit, overhauling them at Wellington, driving them from the town. They made a stand after crossing the Sni. We on approaching the bridge made no halt, driving and scattering the enemy in every direction, killing many of them, we having one man (Lieutenant Ferd Scott) wounded in the side. As usual, they could not stand our onslaught.[19]

After the fight was over, we marched west to Macklin, where we stopped for supper. Finding that Burris was still in pursuit, we moved our camp three miles north, where we rested until morning. About daybreak the next morning we moved to Bone Hill, where we got breakfast, but we had barely finished when our pickets were driven in by Burris. This time Colonel Burris pressed us more vigorously but did not bring us to a stand until about four o'clock p.m. on the high prairie north from Pleasant Hill, where we lost one man, young Simmons from Westport. I never knew if

---

19. James Christian, Union captain, confirmed Gregg's account that these Union soldiers were paroled and not executed despite Halleck's order that refused guerrillas the same protections. See *O.R.*, series 2, vol. 4, 721. For more on the action described here, see the September 24, 1862, report by Lieutenant Colonel John T. Burris in *O.R.*, series 1, vol. 13, 267–68. Harvey Gleaves was a wealthy Virginia-born farmer. His combined wealth was nearly $33,000 in 1860. See Federal Manuscript Census, Lafayette County, Mo., 320. The man wounded here, Ferdinand Scott, was a prominent guerrilla who began the war fighting on the north side of the Missouri River in Clay County with Frank James and other Clay County boys.

we did the enemy any damage. On reaching the timber we scattered our men in order to avoid pursuit, which we did very effectually.

After a rest of four or five days, the boys were together again, fresh and ready for the fray, and the fray was soon upon us. Camped in the river bottom one mile below Sibley, 150 of Penick's cutthroats drove our pickets in who were stationed in town. Although our force was only one hundred strong, we decided to give them battle, and, believing they would go south to the Lexington and Independence road, we at once repaired to that road, arriving at the farmhouse of Mrs. Garrison and the road leading north to Sibley. We halted for a short consultation with Colonel Dick Chiles, who had that day fallen in with us. He asked to be given a command of the advance, to which Quantrill said, "no, I do not know you, I do not know if you would carry out my instructions. Here are my Lieutenants Gregg and Todd, I know that either of them will do just as I tell them." The lieutenants spoke up and said, "Let him have it." So Quantrill said to Chiles, "you must obey these orders. When you meet the enemy, you must not stop, but go right into them, I will be there to support you, now go."[20]

Chiles moved out gaily and briskly with twenty-five as brave and dauntless soldiers as ever followed any man, and Chiles was no coward. But unfortunately for poor Chiles, he disobeyed the orders given by our dauntless commander. When he met the enemy, he stopped and dismounted his men, giving the enemy time to dismount, take possession of a log house and heavy rail fence. Soon after Chiles dismounted, he was shot through the lungs, from which he never recovered. Quantrill saw at a glance that it was useless to continue the fight. So he called the men off, carrying Chiles to the home of Mrs. Garrison, where we left him. He also had one man wounded, Pat O'Donnell.[21]

Soon after the Sibley affair, which was late in September 1862, we planned and carried out another successful raid on Kansas. This time, Shawnee Town was the objective point. This was to have been a bloodless affair, but unfortunately we struck a train of wagons on the Santa Fe Trail, guarded by a troop of infantry. This infantry was taken by surprise. They

20. Colonel William R. Penick led the Fifth Missouri Cavalry, Missouri State Militia, which was very active in the fighting along the border. Lieutenant Colonel Richard B. Chiles was an officer in the First Missouri Cavalry, Confederate States Army, before he resigned to fight as a guerrilla.

21. As his name would imply, Pat O'Donnell was Irish born. He worked as a shoemaker in Independence and was married with three young children in 1860. See the 1860 Federal Manuscript Census, Jackson County, Mo., 247.

had gone to sleep without a camp guard, much less a picket. As soon as they were wakened, there was a general scramble to get away and I think that about half escaped, but the others were shot down as they ran. This raid was planned for the purpose of securing clothing for the men; however, it was almost a water haul for Shawnee Town was possessed of but little of that commodity. This Shawnee Town raid was made about the twentieth of October.

The last mentioned affair was about the last escapade of Quantrill in the Missouri River country in 1862. What little time we remained after that we devoted to preparations for the trip south, which began on the sixth day of November, our rendezvous being on Big Creek, Cass County, Missouri—not far from the scene of the Searaucy battle. We struck the Harrisonville and Holden road about sundown in the evening, our advance striking a train of U.S. wagons escorted by about forty Iowa Cavalry. Quantrill ordered Lieutenant Gregg to advance with forty men and attack the cavalcade. We captured the train which was drawn by cattle. The enemy corralled the wagons and tried to enter the corral, but Gregg was too quick for them. Nearly every one of forty was either killed or captured.[22]

Some two miles south from where we captured this train, we camped, fed, and lunched. Before we moved, our pickets reported the enemy coming, and they actually pushed our pickets on to us before we got out of camp. Captain Harrison being in the rear, we placed a sergeant with ten men as rear guard. The sergeant and men were inexperienced. The enemy drove them pell-mell upon the rear, which was also composed of raw men, stampeding the whole of Harrison's company. We had just arrived at the top of a sharp ridge where Lieutenants Gregg, Todd, and Haller formed all the veterans of Quantrill's old company.[23] Seeing that the enemy's force was far superior to ours in numbers, Lieutenant Gregg ordered his men back from the crest of the ridge, giving a chance to see the enemy by skylight. As soon as the enemy came in view, Gregg ordered a charge. The enemy was surprised and was hurled back at least half a mile. Never daunted, however, they came again each time with increased numbers, but each time they were hurled back with that same impetuous charge directed by Lieutenants Gregg, Todd, and Haller. The third charge, however, was enough, and we resumed our march without the

---

22. *O.R.*, series 1, vol. 13, 781–82.
23. Gregg also spelled Haller's name as "Hallar."

loss of a man killed or wounded. What damage we inflicted on the enemy we never knew definitely.

On our march southward, we chanced to fall in with Colonel Warner Lewis, who had a command of about two hundred men. Lewis insisted that Quantrill should join forces with him in an attack on Lamar, which was finally agreed to on the condition that Lewis would attack simultaneously with us. The hour for the attack being ten o'clock p.m., Lewis was to enter from the north and Quantrill from the south. On nearing the town limits, Quantrill found that he was a few minutes ahead of time, so we halted. We waited for the exact time when we rushed the guards and brought on the fight, in which we lost two men killed and accomplished nothing. Lewis not showing up, we pulled our men off and continued our journey south, passing some miles west from Carthage, turning westward and entering the Indian Territory, going to Fort Smith by way of Gibson.[24]

Arriving at Fort Smith, we were assigned to General Jo O. Shelby's command, taking an active part in battle of Cane Hill, Prairie Grove, Springfield, Hartville, etc. However, before the battle was opened at Cane Hill, Quantrill had obtained leave of absence and started on a journey to Richmond, Virginia, leaving Lieutenant Gregg in command, now being the first lieutenant. Possibly, some may think me ungenerous for relating an occurrence that took place at Cane Hill, but I have said that nothing but the truth was history and that I was going to tell the truth, let the chips fall where they might. When I took command, I noticed that Lieutenant Todd was not about. On close inquiry I found that he with eight men had left for Missouri some hour or so before I made that inquiry. Whether Todd left with consent of Quantrill or not, I was never able to learn.[25]

After the Battle of Hartville, Lieutenant Gregg was given recruiting papers and ordered to the Missouri River by Brigadier General John S. Marmaduke, leaving the skeleton of Quantrill's command in charge of Third Lieutenant Scott. On Quantrill's return from Richmond in the spring, he

---

24. Lewis was an officer in Major General Sterling Price's force, though apparently not a very reliable one. In addition to the above story, Confederate correspondence reveals that in the spring of 1863, when he was set to rendezvous with other Confederate forces in southwestern Missouri, he arrived alone, without his command, which had apparently been overtaken by Indians allied with the Union. See *O.R.*, series 1, vol. 22, part 2, 849–50.

25. Shelby was a wealthy slaveholder before the war, deeply invested in the defense of the institution and protection of his state. O'Flaherty, *General Jo Shelby*. For insight into the guerrillas' time with General Jo Shelby, in particular their role at the Battle of Prairie Grove, see Shelby's report on the battle in *O.R.*, series 1, vol. 22, part 1, 148–54.

brought the skeleton of his command back to the Missouri River, arriving early in May. Owing to the excessively hard winter, Lieutenant Gregg's operations were limited until March, when with eleven men he captured the government steamer *Sam Gaty* near Sibley, destroying half a million dollars in sugar, coffee, flour, bacon, et cetera, and killing some fourteen soldiers of Penick's command.[26]

On Quantrill's return to the state, military operations began in earnest, however, on a different line from the previous year. During the year 1862 the men were kept close together and all under the watchful eye of Quantrill. Not so in 1863. There was Todd, Pool, Blunt, Younger, Anderson, and others, and each had companies and were only called together on special occasions. All of whom, however, recognized Quantrill as commander in chief, with Lieutenant Gregg as adjutant. Occurrences were thick and fast during the summer of 1863. Todd would annihilate a party of the enemy in western Jackson County. Blunt another in the eastern portion, Anderson somewhere in Kansas or Cass County, Missouri, Pool in Lafayette or Saline, Younger on the High Blue. Some one of these commanders were in collision with the enemy almost every day up to about the first of August, when the enemy ceased its activity from some cause or other, giving Quantrill and his men much-needed rest.

About June 5, 1863, Lieutenants Gregg and Scott with eight men crossed the Missouri River to Ray County. In Clay County there was a militia captain, Sessions, who had been terrorizing the Southern citizens, several of whom he had murdered. So, this raid was concocted for the purpose of getting Captain Sessions. Gregg and Scott moved within one mile of Missouri City (where Sessions was stationed with a troop of soldiers), camped, made arrangements with an old farmer to report to Sessions that there were two drunken bushwhackers at his place, menacing his family. Gregg put Scott in charge of eight men, placed them in ambush with instructions to let the enemy pass his position before firing. Gregg and James Little remained mounted. The farmer reported

---

26. Not unlike Shelby, James Marmaduke was a wealthy planter before the war. After the war, he became the governor of Missouri, his election being viewed as a redemption of the old slaveholding Democratic Party that had dominated state politics before the war. The attack on the *Sam Gaty* occurred on March 28, 1863. Gregg does not mention that among the men killed were anywhere between nine and twenty "contrabands," or black men who were probably in the service of the army as laborers but may have been soldiers. The tone of the Union reports suggest they were unarmed and executed in an act of racial violence not dissimilar to more notable events like the one at Fort Pillow. See *O.R.*, series 1, vol. 22, part 1, 245–46; part 2, 183, 194–95, 203.

Sessions came with eleven men, supposing the two drunken men was all he would have to contend with. Gregg had told Scott to be sure to kill the two foremost men and he would get Sessions, the two mounted men [Gregg and Little] being concealed by Pawpaw bushes. Sessions was soon there. Scott followed instructions to the letter, but instead of only killing the two foremost, he killed eight and wounded the ninth one. Gregg and Little killed the three who were unhurt in the ambush. Moving on the town, at once, we procured a large Union flag, which we found locked in an iron safe that was soon opened by the use of a sledgehammer procured from a nearby blacksmith shop.[27]

At sundown Gregg resumed his march to northern Clay County in search of recruits. Arriving at the house of a Mr. Soper early the next morning, we hid the men and horses in a wooded pasture where we lay until four o'clock p.m., when we repaired to the house for supper. Schoolchildren stopping at the house told of seeing troops pass south on the Liberty and Plattsburg road, only two hundred yards away. Believing these to be troops from Plattsburg, Gregg determined to take that town also. Moving within four miles of Plattsburg that night and sleeping 'til near twelve next day, Gregg sent spies in and found that twenty militia had been left to guard the place with three hundred loaded guns in the courthouse. Gregg, knowing the soldiers were not on the lookout, determined to march in quietly and take possession of the courthouse. Lieutenant Scott and Joe Hart, the latter having fallen in with us at Soper's, objected to Gregg's plan and proposed that we divide the men, allowing six men to make a charge on the courthouse shooting in the air to scare the militia away. "Yes," said Gregg, "you will scare them into the courthouse." By this time we were in the suburbs, had captured Colonel Jim Burch, aide-de-camp to Governor Hamilton Gamble. Gregg said, "Well boys, there are two against me. I will accept your plan and lead the charge."[28]

---

27. *O.R.*, series 1, vol. 22, part 1, 335–36. Union authorities describe the ambush as a much smaller affair with only a handful of Union troops involved. Also, they offer a much gorier picture of what it meant to "get" Sessions.

28. According to the 1860 Federal Manuscript Census, Clay County, Mo., there are two Soper households. Both households were located in Platte Township, and they appear on consecutive pages of the census. On p. 222 is John Soper's household, and on p. 223 is Benjamin Soper's household. Benjamin Soper was likely John's father, as Benjamin was seventy years old in 1860, and John was thirty-five. It is unclear at which household Gregg and his band stayed in 1863. The guerrilla Joe Hart became a somewhat infamous lothario after the war and even beyond the Missouri theater of the guerrilla war when his diary appeared in a national publication. See *Harper's Weekly*, December 16, 1865.

Joe Hart, John Jackson, Henry Cowherd (cousin to the present congressman), Jim Little, and Fletch Taylor volunteered to go with Gregg. When within two blocks of the courthouse they began shooting in the air and on reaching the square received a volley from the court house. Henry Cowherd's horse fell at the corner of the square, putting him hors de combat. Jackson, Taylor, and Little dashed by the courthouse, receiving a galling fire from the enemy within. Gregg, riding a three-year-old unbroken mare, stopped immediately in front of the courthouse and drove the enemy from the windows. But where was Joe Hart? One of the men who proposed this plan of attack? Hidden behind the buildings west of the courthouse. When Gregg had driven the enemy from the windows on the west side, they repaired to the windows on the north and began a fusillade at Jackson, Taylor, and Little, who were sitting on their horses at the northwest corner of the square. Gregg at once ordered Little to go to the north side of the courthouse, drive the enemy away from the windows, and hold the position until Scott came up with the remainder of our men, when, Gregg said, "we will storm and take the courthouse." Little, a brave, dauntless fellow, obeyed the order at once, drove the enemy away, when they surrendered on condition that they were not to be shot. The men captured at the courthouse and Colonel Burch being paroled, we proceeded to destroy the guns found in the courthouse.

Leaving Plattsburg near sundown in the evening, Gregg with James A. Hendricks repaired to Platte County in quest of some twenty men who he had sworn into the service early in the spring, leaving Lieutenant Scott in charge. On Gregg's arrival in Platte, he found his recruits had gone on the plains. Hence there was nothing to do but return to his command. On the return, arriving at Smithville, located on Smiths Fork of the Platte River, they found the town full of militia. Passing through the town and the militia unnoticed, arriving at the bridge, which was a covered structure, their horses refused to enter. Being very dark they could not see in the bridge. A flash of lightning disclosed the trouble: the bridge was full of sleeping militia. Hendricks's horse fell, leaving him behind. Gregg managed to take Hendricks's horse back through the town, where he waited for Hendricks, who soon appeared, arriving at camp the next morning all safe.

By this time, north Missouri had been thoroughly aroused. All the federals stationed in striking distance had been set in motion to capture the ten men who had dared to cross the Missouri River, capture two towns, and defy ten thousand Federal troops. Besides, we had killed the pitted Sessions and eleven men. Sending two men to the locality where we had crossed the river to secure a skiff, Gregg marched by easy stages to an obscure crossing on Fishing River. Arriving there at dawn, posting a picket on our trail, he sent two men to the Missouri to find a way to cross. In two hours they returned begrimed and powder burnt; they were ambushed by infantry on the bank of the Missouri. They were otherwise unscathed. Not to be outdone, Gregg sent two men to Sibley in search of the two men he sent to secure a skiff. They too returned without success. Near sundown, while the men were all asleep, our picket reported the enemy coming on our trail. All was hurry scurry, but before we could move, the enemy was in our camp. They did not seem to recognize that we were an enemy and did not fire on us until we had crossed Fishing River. After fighting for some time, five of Gregg's men became separated from him. Gregg fooled the enemy by turning north and going back to Kearny, near the famous Samuels residence. From there he went to Blue Mill landing, where he constructed a raft and recrossed the Missouri. On launching the raft, however, they found the water only six inches deep for nearly one hundred yards. This was at one o'clock in the morning, and they reached floating water at sunrise, with a steamer in sight.[29]

The enemy had been more savage, if possible, than ever before. They had killed numerous old men and boys. One boy, son of Henry Morris, was only eleven years old. There could have been no better argument for the people to flock to Quantrill than the dastardly acts of the enemy and they came. About August 10, 1863, Quantrill called his various captains together for a council of war, which lasted near twenty-four hours. Quantrill said, "Let's go to Lawrence," and in support of this proposition he said, "Lawrence is the great hotbed of abolitionism in Kansas and all the plunder (or the bulk of it) stolen from Missouri will be found stored away in Lawrence, and we can get more revenge and more money there than anywhere else in the state." Some said that the undertaking was too hazardous. "I know," said the chief, "but if you never risk you will never gain." So Quantrill won. Quantrill and his captains busied themselves the next five or six days in having the men prepare an extra supply of ammunition but did not tell the men of the contemplated raid.[30]

---

29. *O.R.*, series 1, vol. 22, part 1, 335–36. The Samuels residence was the home of Jesse and Frank James. Their mother Zerelda had married a Dr. Reuben Samuels after her first husband, the boys' father, had died.

30. In the 1860 Federal Manuscript Census, Jackson County, Henry Morris was listed as a wagon maker who had moved to Missouri around ten years earlier from Tennessee. Henry and his wife, Martha, had six children, ranging from age one to thirteen, at the time of the census. John, who Gregg references being killed, was listed as being nine years old in 1860.

Why did we make the raid to Lawrence? Jennison, Lane, Burris, and many other marauding bands under leaders of lesser border fame had visited various Missouri border counties and never left the state without murdering, plundering, and devastating the houses of a greater or less number of our citizens. To kill, it was only necessary to know that a man sympathized with the South, but as to robbing, they robbed everybody without distinction and they often laid waste whole districts. I counted thirteen houses burning at one time on January 28, 1862. This burning was done by Jennison's men. Although government officials said Jennison was not a U.S. officer and had no authority, he carried the U.S. flag and was often assisted in his forays by troops stationed at Independence and other stations in Jackson and adjoining counties. These parties until early in 1863 did not haul away much household plunder, contenting themselves with such as blankets, quilts, wearing apparel, and jewelry. Such articles they could carry on their horses, but they usually went back to Kansas well-loaded with such articles as I have mentioned.[31]

It would be too tedious for me in this brief history to mention all the atrocious acts of the Kansan, combined with Federal troops stationed in Missouri, though many of the troops stationed in Missouri were Kansans. Hence I will give you one circumstance in illustration of a hundred other similar ones. About February 18, 1863, Colonel Bill Penick, stationed at Independence and whose men were part Missourians and part Kansans, sent a scout of about seventy-five men sixteen miles southeast of Independence to the houses of Colonel Jim Saunders and Uncle Jeptha Crawford. The scout, arriving at the house of Saunders first, divided, one-half going to Crawford's. Mrs. Saunders and her daughter prepared dinner for the half stopping there. The colonel furnished feed for their horses, and all went well until dinner was over. Mind you, the snow was fourteen inches deep with the mercury ten below zero when Colonel Saunders was placed under guard and the house burned with the women not allowed a bonnet or shawl. On leaving Saunders's place, they told his wife they were going to take the colonel to Independence and make him take the oath. On the arrival of this party at Crawford's, practically the same

---

31. A letter written in February 1862, O. G. Cates called Secretary of War Edwin Stanton to put a stop to the atrocities committed by Kansas troops—"thief[s] and jayhawker[s]"—which would seem to confirm the environment described by Gregg even in early 1862 in *O.R.*, series 1, vol. 27, part 2, 93–94. According to the 1860 U.S. Federal Manuscript Census, Jackson County, Cates was a wealthy lawyer living in Independence. For a history of jayhawkers see Benedict, *Jayhawkers.*

scenes were enacted except they snatched a lace cap from the head of Mrs. Crawford and threw it in the flames of the burning building. They also told Mrs. Crawford that the men would not be hurt. On their way to Independence, arriving at the house of James Burris, they dismounted Crawford and Saunders and shot them to death. It was such dastardly acts as the foregoing that caused the raid on Lawrence.[32]

On August 18, 1863, the bulk of Quantrill's forces met on Little Sni Creek, in the Cummings settlement, twenty-four miles southeast from Independence. From there we went to Captain Perdee's place on the Blackwater River in Johnson County, Missouri, where all the men met. There Quantrill and his officers held a council of war. When it was determined (circumstances admitting) we would go to Lawrence, the men were then informed of the contemplated raid. Quantrill told them of the great hazard of the trip and that the entire command stood a chance of being annihilated and that all who felt they were not equal to the herculean task ought not undertake it and that any man who refused to go would not be censured. Leaving Captain Perdee's place, we marched in the direction of Lone Jack with a cordon of videttes in every direction from our little army of 294 men, rank and file.[33]

These videttes were charged to keep a sharp lookout for the enemy. We marched very slowly, the videttes reporting every few minutes that there was no enemy in sight. When the day was nearly gone and we had only made ten miles, the videttes were all called in, all giving the same report: no enemy sighted. The circumstances were a thing of the past, the raid to Lawrence was assured. We stopped for one hour, getting a bite to eat and feeding our horses. We then began the march in earnest. Arriving on the headwaters of the Grand River at five o'clock on August 20, we lay concealed in the timber until 3:30 p.m., when we again resumed our march to Lawrence. Crossing the state line within a half mile of Aubury, where two hundred Federal troops were quartered in the bright sunlight of the evening. These troops rode out on the prairie, formed, and looked at us pass. Not a man of ours broke ranks. Not a shot fired, we marched in a northwesterly direction, halting at dusk to graze our horses. This portion

32. While there is no corroborating evidence of this raid in the *O.R.*, other documents reveal Penick's awareness of the significance of the household and of women in particular to the guerrilla war effort. See *O.R.*, series 1, vol. 22, part 1, 244.

33. Captain Perdee was James Perdee, a sixty-year-old Virginia-born farmer who had moved to Missouri in the mid-1830s. See 1860 Federal Manuscript Census, Johnson County, Mo.

of Kansas was sparsely settled at this time. We crossed the old Santa Fe Trail at Spring Hill, where we saw on the streets several Federal soldiers in uniform but did not molest them or make any stop in the place.[34]

We had now arrived at a point where none of our men knew the country; hence it became necessary to procure a guide. Every one procured, however, chanced to be known by one of our men and was shot. Things went on this way until probably ten men had been killed. We were nearing the Wakarusa River and were within twelve or thirteen miles of Lawrence when we procured another guide who was recognized by Todd, but orders had been issued that there should be no more shooting. So a musket was brought forth with which the man was clubbed to death. Having reached the Wakarusa timbers, Quantrill recognized the country and led the way himself.[35]

Having entered the Wakarusa timbers within four or five miles of Franklin, the crowing of the cock warned us of the near approach of daylight. It being our desire to reach Lawrence not later than sunrise, the horses were hurried to a long trot, reaching Franklin just at dawn. As we yet had five miles to cover, the men were thrown into a column of fours and put to a gallop. On reaching the summit of a ridge lying midway between Franklin and Lawrence, Quantrill ordered Lieutenant Gregg to advance with five men and learn if there was any considerable force to oppose us. On reaching a suburb south of the main town, Lieutenant Gregg and his party came upon a camp of about forty tents. Waiting for the main command to come up, Lieutenant Gregg and his party killed several soldiers, among them a boy about eighteen years of age and supposed to be orderly to some general. On arrival of the command, Lieutenant Gregg fell in beside Quantrill, who was at the head of the column. Pointing toward the camp, Quantrill and Lieutenant Gregg did not stop but turned to the east to Massachusetts Street, up which they bolted at breakneck speed. The command on reaching the open space in which the tents were standing deployed right and left and charged the camp, and in three minutes there was not a tent standing nor a man alive in camp. Quantrill's order was to kill, kill, and you will make no mistake, Lawrence is the hotbed and should be thoroughly cleansed, and the only way to cleanse it is to kill.

---

34. A vidette is simply a picket on horseback.

35. According to Connelley, the man who was brutally clubbed to death was Joseph Stone, "a refuge from Missouri" who had prompted the arrest of George Todd early in the war. Recognizing Stone, Todd was the man who bashed in Stone's brains. See Connelley, *Quantrill and the Border Wars*, 326–27.

The killing finished, the men were ordered to burn the town. Quantrill said, give the Kansas people a taste of what the Missourian has suffered at the hands of the Kansas jayhawker. Lieutenant Gregg relates this story of what he saw and burned at Lawrence: when the order was given to burn, I repaired to the southern portion of the main town, where I found about forty shanties, built with three sides boards, the fourth a hay stack, and covered with hay. All of these shacks were filled with household effects stolen from Missouri. Much we recognized—many of these had feather beds, quilts, blankets, et cetera stacked in them higher than I could reach, fine bed stands, bureaus, sideboards, bookcases, and pianos that cost thousands of dollars. These shacks were in the charge of negro women, many of whom we recognized. One negro woman, I recollect distinctly, was the property of Colonel Steel, who lived near Sibley in Jackson County, Missouri.[36]

The town burnt, the men were collected and orders given to move out. Lieutenant Gregg was given orders to take twenty men, scour the place, and see that every man was gotten out. However, one man escaped the vigilance of this guard and remained in the place where he soon after met a horrible fate. Mr. J. C. Horton, now a wholesale druggist and honored citizen of Kansas City, Missouri, described the killing of this man (Larkin Skaggs) in this manner: "Yes," said Mr. Horton, "I saw the whole thing. Skaggs rode near a squad of armed men, who shot him off his horse. One of these men got a rope, tied it about Skaggs's neck and about the pummel of his saddle, dragged the dead Skaggs through the streets until the body was nude and terribly mutilated, then hanged the body and further mutilated it by cutting it with knives, shooting and throwing rocks at it, beat it with clubs, et cetera." The question was asked Mr. Horton, "Did Quantrill's men do anything that mean in Lawrence?" To which he said, "They did not."[37]

---

36. According to the 1860 U.S. Federal Census Slave Schedule for Jackson County, Larkin Steel owned six slaves. One of these slaves was a thirty-seven-year-old woman who was likely the woman mentioned by Gregg. Given the age of the other slaves, all of which were twelve years old or younger, it is quite possible that this was a family and that the woman Gregg saw at Lawrence was their mother.

37. Despite Gregg's claim here, the guerrillas did things as brutal and much more so. For example, the guerrillas bound two men together with cords and then threw the pair into a flaming building and watched as they were burned alive. How much brutality Gregg witnessed firsthand is up for debate, as there were hundreds of guerrillas spread over several blocks committing acts of a varying range of violence. Nevertheless, Gregg paints too pretty a picture of his fellow killers. See Richard Cordley, letter to the congressional record, found at Richard Cordley, "A History of Lawrence, Kansas," Kansas Collection Books,

Mr. Horton was captured at the Eldridge Hotel and by chance was placed under guard with a bunch of Lawrence people who were being protected by Quantrill. Otherwise, Mr. Horton might have been killed also. This wholesale killing was repugnant to many of the men and also many of the officers, but forbearance had ceased to be a virtue. Our own loved ones had been murdered, robbed, and insulted. There was a price upon the head of Quantrill and every one of his men. Anderson's sisters had been murdered, and any day any of our sisters were liable to be murdered. Yet, Mr. Horton says, "if there was a woman or child harmed by Quantrill's men at Lawrence, I never heard of it." On leaving Lawrence, Quantrill halted four miles south of the town on the Osawatomie road at a farm house, giving ample time for all of the stragglers to overtake the command. Except for Larkin Skaggs, all reported. I have omitted mention of the fact that Lieutenant Bledsoe was wounded at Lawrence. Shot by a federal across the Kaw, this man we hauled to Missouri in an ambulance.[38]

I want to say that Quantrill and his men had gotten safely to Lawrence and accomplished their purpose, but getting safely back to Missouri was another proposition. The entire state of Kansas was aroused, as if by magic. The wires had told the news of the sacking and burning of Lawrence to thirty thousand Federal troops in Missouri. At Black Jack Point, eight miles south of Lawrence, we encountered the enemy, seven hundred strong. We at once halted for a council. It was determined we should continue south until all was in readiness, then turn east for Missouri. The enemy, seeing that our number was much less than theirs, advanced and opened fire on our rear. At this juncture Quantrill cut out 100 men, attacked, and whipped the enemy in five minutes. Returning, Quantrill ordered Gregg to cut out 60 men and hold the rear until the main command had crossed a small river one mile away. When the call for the 60 men was made, 150 responded; however, only 60 were permitted to remain. Gregg with his 60 men remained stationary until the main command had disappeared in the timber. When Gregg slowly retreated, having passed the timber, Quantrill was found waiting but had turned

---

1895, http://www.kancoll.org/books/cordley_massacre/quantrel.raid.html; Goodrich, *Black Flag,* 77–95.

    38. William Bledsoe was a twenty-five-year-old carpenter's apprentice living in Independence when the war began. Just like the other officers, he was a bit older than the typical guerrilla. See 1860 U.S. Federal Manuscript Census, Jackson County, Mo.

to the east. On approaching the command, Lieutenant Gregg received these orders from Quantrill: "Form your sixty men in skirmish line and hold the rear. Fall back on me whenever it may be necessary, but whatever you do, don't let them break your line." However, before Gregg had completed his skirmish line, the enemy, now 1,200 strong, was upon him, and the battle was on.

The fighting had continued about one hour when the enemy pushed Gregg with his heroic little band upon our main line. Our little army, less than one-fourth the enemy, then faced about, charged the Kansans, and drove them back. Lieutenant Gregg and his sixty men then took their place in the rear as before, holding their position up to four o'clock p.m. Having held the rear for five hours against a force five thousand strong, the scene was an ominous one—a sea of prairie, not a tree or twig to be seen. Reinforcements flocked to the enemy by companies and by regiments; it really looked as though we were doomed. The whole earth was blue behind us. Lieutenant Gregg became exhausted, his voice failed him. He reported to Quantrill his condition at once. The heroic Todd was ordered to take his place, and he continued to hold the enemy in check. Like Wellington at Waterloo, we prayed that night that succor might come. Thus the fight went on until near sundown. We came in sight of Paola, where in the broad sunlight glittered the guns of 1,500 cavalry. We were near timbered heights of Bull Creek, and the enemy could see this force as well as we and it emboldened them. They rushed Todd's line, driving him upon the main line. "Halt!" said Quantrill. "Face about!" The men faced about; not a single man disobeyed with the enemy at sixty yards. "Steady men. . . . Charge!" rang out upon the Kansas breeze. The men charged. The enemy stood. Our men were thinning their ranks. The enemy was falling thick and fast. Their line began to break. Quantrill ordered another charge. Our boys went at them again and drove them pell-mell like a drove of sheep for half a mile or more.

The fight in Kansas was ended.

We marched from there to the headwaters of the Grand River in Cass County, Missouri, where we arrived at 5:30 a.m. on August 22, 1863. In all this fighting, we covered a distance of more than twenty-five miles. The fighting never ceased for a single moment. Yet this little band of heroes came out of it all unscathed, not a man of them being touched. Under all these trials, I never saw but one man falter and that man was Joab Perry. A little after four o'clock in the evening, Joe became panic stricken. He struck out alone, his long hair standing out in the Kansas breeze. Some of the men wanted to kill him, while others said, "no, he will get it soon enough," but he made it through to Missouri unscathed so far as bullets were concerned. He was, however, horseless, bootless, coat-less, and with only one revolver out of six. The remainder of his clothing was torn to shreds; his flesh terribly mutilated by brush and briar. In all this fighting Quantrill only lost one man killed, and he was entirely hid from them by a ridge when killed.

We camped on a prominence on the headwaters of Grand River and sent men among the farmers to get provisions for the men. But before it could be procured, the Kansans were in sight with greatly augmented numbers. At this juncture a laughable incident occurred. Quantrill had been informed by a citizen whom we met that 1,200 federals awaited him just over the divide four miles away, but he had not told the men. Quan-trill mounted his horse, rode through the camp, and ordered the men to saddle up. "What for?" said the men. "Why," he said, "the Kansans are coming." "*Damn* the Kansans" came from a hundred or more voices, "we whipped them yesterday, we can whip them today, and we are not going to leave here till we get something to eat." "Yes," said Quantrill. "I know you can whip the Kansans, but what are you going to do about the 1,200 fresh Missouri troops awaiting us just over the divide?" "Well," said they, "that is a horse of another color, we will saddle up," and they did.

In one hour or less time the command dwindled away by at least one-third. Bledsoe, the man wounded at Lawrence and brought through in an ambulance, was sent to the timber where he was soon after killed. So many horses were broken down that the men were compelled to take to the timber. Sure enough, Quantrill met the federals just over the divide, skirmished with them, and scattered his men. No men were lost, but sev-eral horses were. Thus, you might say, ended the Lawrence raid, but not our troubles by any means. The Federal government had thirty thousand troops in search of us, watching the roads, stream crossings, and many dwelling houses. In the next five or six days, we lost more men than we lost on the Lawrence raid.[39]

It was soon after the Lawrence raid that the famous Order No. 11 was issued by the monster of monsters, General Tom Ewing, under which the border counties of Missouri from the river south were depopulated and

---

39. For Union reports on Quantrill's raid of Lawrence, Kansas, see *O.R.*, series 1, vol. 22, part 1, 576–93.

made a desert. No people ever suffered so much as the people of Jackson County did under this order. Being forced to leave in a specified time, it was impossible for them to move but little of their plunder, provisions, et cetera. It was a gruesome sight to see these people on the move, some with their cows or an old plug horse or jennet packed. The women and children on foot left behind plenty of corn, hogs, chickens, and turkeys, et cetera, thousands of bushels of corn in the crib, besides what was in the field, many of them without a dollar. All of this wealth left by these people was either burned or appropriated by the Federal government or the Kansan and these people never received a single cent from any source. Yet in the eyes of the people of the North, there were no demons but Quantrill and his men. As I told a reporter for the Saint Louis *Globe Democrat*, Quantrill and his men went to Lawrence with hell in their necks and raised hell after they got there.[40]

I have a blame to lay to Quantrill for some things that he permitted at Lawrence. Of course he could not have his eye on every man, for the men were scattered promiscuously over the town. But he told me in support of his argument for the raid that there was a great deal of money there, "and," said he, "I want to compensate the people who have and still will divide their last biscuit with us." "Well," said I in reply, "that is very laudable." "Now," said Quantrill, "my plan is that whatever money that may be gotten at Lawrence will be divided among the men with instructions to give to those people very liberally." But on our return this prorate division was never mentioned. The truth is that Quantrill tried to manage so that Todd and his men would get the money. It happened, however, that Charley Higbee secured the largest sum of any one man, who immediately after our return to Missouri left for parts unknown to us at the time. It was reported afterwards that he went to Canada. Soon after the close of the war, we heard of Higbee at Fort Worth, Texas, in the banking business. In the eyes of the survivors of Quantrill's band and the people of Missouri, he was a traitor.[41]

---

40. For the complete transcription of Ewing's General Order 11, see *O.R.*, series 1, vol. 22, part 2, 473.

41. In the original text, Gregg spelled the name of this traitor both "Higbie" and "Higbee." I determined to use the latter because there are only Higbees in western Missouri at the outset of the war. The 1860 Federal Manuscript Census, Jackson County, shows a twenty-three-year-old H. C. Higbee who had been born in Kentucky and was a wealthy lawyer living in the Jones Hotel in Independence in 1860.

Between the time of the consummation of the Lawrence Raid and the first of October, there was but little doing. There seemed to be a lull after the country was depopulated on the part of the Federal soldiery. Whatever was done was of minor importance. So I will pass on to our march to Texas, beginning about October 1, 1863. Our rendezvous being at Captain Perdee's in Johnson County, Missouri, our march was practically due south to or beyond Carthage and without incident. Turning a southwesterly course there, we crossed Spring River into Kansas. Quantrill's command at this time was composed of four companies: Pool, Todd/Anderson, Gregg, and Younger. They ranged from thirty to eighty men to the company, with quite a sprinkling of recruits going to the Confederate Army, amounting in all to about four hundred men.

It so happened on the day we crossed into Kansas that Pool, who had thirty men, was in advance, and Gregg with thirty men was in the rear. On crossing Spring River, Pool encountered several wagons and teams driven by Federal soldiers. There teamsters told Pool that there was a Federal camp at Baxter Springs. When this information was communicated to Quantrill, he at once ordered Gregg to the front, sending him immediately to Pool's support, who was within fifty yards of the Federal camp and fooling the enemy by hoisting a small Federal flag. Quantrill said to Gregg, "Support Pool. I will come in on the north and support both of you." On arrival at Pool's position, Gregg fell in on the right, fronting west and immediately abutting a long, low cabin built of unhewn logs. The order to charge was at once given. Gregg was crowded to the right of the cabin with three men, where to their surprise they found a formidable fort of earthworks.

On the commencement of this attack, about twenty-five of the enemy ran away about two hundred yards and hid under the grass and willows. Thinking Pool was master of the situation, Gregg took two men to capture these men hidden in the slough. After a few moments, Gregg and his two men had pulled twenty of the runaways from their hiding. Noticing the firing about the fort had ceased, with an occasional bullet whizzing about him, Gregg mounted his horse to investigate. He found the enemy advancing from the fort, with none of his comrades in sight. On riding to the crest of the ridge to the north, Gregg found Quantrill confronting Major General James G. Blunt with an escort of about 150 men, a band, a small wagon train, an ambulance, a buggy, et cetera. Gregg and his two men left their twenty prisoners, made a dash for Quantrill's line. Shot at from three different quarters, it looked almost like a forlorn hope, though they reached Quantrill unscathed. A charge was ordered, with instructions to hold fire until in fifty yards. However, the enemy did not wait for us to get so near but fired and broke pell-mell over the prairie, which seemed endless in the direction they were forced to.[42]

The greater portion of Blunt's party was annihilated in less time than it takes to write it. Major Curtis, Blunt's adjutant general, and the son of Major General Curtis were among the slain. Stories to the contrary notwithstanding, the men killed in this engagement, with the exception of the bandsmen and driver, were killed in actual combat. In all probability they too would have been so killed only for this reason. William Bledsoe, an excellent soldier, loved, pitied, and honored by Quantrill and all his men, rode to this band, drawn by four mules, and demanded a surrender. Instead of obeying Bledsoe's summons, they shot him to death. Captains Todd and Gregg were in a position to see Bledsoe killed, with about twenty men closed in on this band wagon containing thirteen men. Before reaching the wagon, the left front wheel broke off, precipitating the men to the ground and bringing the wagon to a standstill. All of the men in the wagon began waving their white kerchiefs in token of surrender. Todd and others shouted at them to know why they had not waved their kerchiefs at Bledsoe. The band men were all killed on the spot, and many valuable arms were captured in this little fight, all of which were given to the unarmed. I have since been informed that only about twenty of Blunt's party escaped, General Blunt being among this number.

Our losses were three killed and one wounded. We captured General Blunt's flag, the finest I ever saw, inscribed, "Presented to Maj. Gen. James G. Blunt by the Ladies of Leavenworth Oct 2nd 1863." Quantrill sent the flag to Major General Price. We also got General Blunt's buggy with a span of guns, saddle, commission as major general, ambulance, et cetera. At the conclusion of this battle, Todd and Anderson both insisted that we should storm and take the fort, but Quantrill said, "No, there is nothing to be gained by taking it. Besides," he said, "we would probably loose fifteen or twenty men, and I would not give the life of one of my men for the whole business." We communicated with the fort by flag

---

42. Stiles, *Jesse James*, 100; Castel and Goodrich, *Bloody Bill Anderson*, 31–33. Blunt was a New Englander, political radical, and a migrant to Kansas, where he was a Free State partisan and fighter before the war. He had some early successes in the war on the border and proved to be a solid leader after the Battle of Baxter Springs. See Gerteis, *The Civil War in Missouri*, 147–48, 196–98.

of truce, the only time the Federal authorities ever recognized a flag of truce from us.

Our march from Baxter Springs to Sherman, Texas, was uninterrupted. After resting a few days at Sherman, Quantrill established a camp fifteen miles northwest from there. It was here that the disintegration of Quantrill's command began. Pool, Jarrette, Younger, and Gregg left, taking with them altogether about forty men, most of whom were old tried and true veterans. Gregg joined Shelby and was given a company. Pool, Jarrette, and Younger joined forces and formed a company. Quantrill remained in Texas until about March 15, 1864, when he again turned his eyes toward the Missouri River. However, his ranks were sadly thinned. But a few of the men who had been most instrumental in building the fame of Quantrill were to be seen in his ranks now. Quantrill and Todd came together with forty or fifty men; Anderson with thirty or forty. Their hardships were many. They swam almost every stream from the Red River to the Missouri, and to cap the climax Quantrill and Todd quarreled and parted company before they reached the Missouri. Quantrill with a few chosen friends spent the summer in Howard County, Missouri—you might say, dormant. It really began to look as though Quantrill's military sun had set to rise no more forever.[43]

Captain Todd and Anderson made some good fights this summer. Todd fought the second Colorado at Grinter's farm south of Independence, almost annihilating them notwithstanding they outnumbered Todd. This was a hand-to-hand grapple in which the brave Wagoner and his sturdy brave Coloradans were worsted. Anderson fought at Shaw's shop in Ray County, where he almost annihilated a troop of militia. Todd and Anderson combined fought at Centralia, demolishing Colonel Johnson with three hundred men, allowing only about six men to escape. Quantrill joined with Todd and Anderson at Fayette, although he advised against the attack. It was disastrous; it came out as Quantrill said. Centralia was the last real battle fought by guerrillas in Missouri, though Todd joined forces with Price on his arrival at Lexington, doing scout and advance duty to Independence, where he was killed. Anderson was killed in Ray County soon after. Todd and Anderson were much alike, both brave to a fault, maniacs in battle, with no regard for the lives of their men. I

---

43. Younger confirms the departure of these men, more or less. See Younger, *The Story of Cole Younger*, 61–63.

have often seen them cry and froth at the mouth in battle, simply because they could not kill a whole regiment of the enemy in a few minutes. Not so with Quantrill, who had the greatest care for the lives of his men. He was always himself in battle and just as brave as Todd or Anderson.[44]

After Price had retired from the state, Quantrill came to Lafayette County, collected about forty men, and started on his famous march to Kentucky. In this little band were Frank James, James Little, Chat Renick, John Barker, Peyton Long, William Bassham, Jack Graham, James Younger, Dick Glasscock, Billy Gaugh, John Barnhill, Hiram Guest, and others whom I do not now remember. This move proved fatal to the far found Quantrill and many of his best men. Being in a strange land among strange people, they were sorely beset. After resorting to subterfuge, dressing in Federal uniform, and passing as federals for days and even weeks at a time, and some time after General Lee had surrendered, Quantrill called his men together some forty miles from Louisville. While encamped in a barnyard, they were then attacked by overwhelming numbers, routed, and several men were killed. Quantrill was so severely wounded that he was able to be moved only to the nearest house, where he fell into the hands of the enemy. From there he was taken to the hospital in Louisville, where he died soon after. Thus ended the career of the much hunted, more feared, far famed William Clarke Quantrill. Although Quantrill and I had some disagreements, I will ever hold his memory sacred. I find many of my old comrades averse to telling of these differences. I, to the contrary, want them known because they are history, and true history can never be recorded and stand the test without recording the facts.

Shortly before Quantrill started for Kentucky, Captain Gregg, who had been on detached service in northern Missouri, recrossed the Missouri River and was married. Quite a number of Quantrill's old men being in the country, they met and organized. Among the number were James A. Hendricks Captain Gregg, and Dick Mattox, all of whom desired to take their wives to Texas. The terms were hastily agreed upon, the men, who

---

44. Although they differ in the troop numbers present, saying that the guerrillas had the superior force, Union officers reported on the skirmish at Grinter's farm. See *O.R.*, series 1, vol. 41, part 1, 49–50. The Wagoner referred to here was Union captain Seymour W. Wagoner. When he said "Colonel Johnson," Gregg was actually referring to Major A. V. E. Johnston, who led between 130 to 140 men at Centralia (not 300). For details of Centralia, see *O.R.*, series 1, vol. 41, part 1, 440–41; Castel and Goodrich, *Bloody Bill Anderson*, 87–98; Stiles, *Jesse James*, 119–27.

were fifty in number, pledging themselves to stand by the three men and their wives. About the tenth day of November, provided with an ambulance loaded with provisions, we made the start at sundown. We marched about thirty miles, camped in the open prairie near Grand River, broke camp at dawn the next morning. Just before entering Grand River Valley, the ambulance came down with a crash. Luckily, however, about one hundred militia were just emerging from the Grand River timbers with several wagons. Our boys made a dash at the militia, drove them away, and captured their wagons. We quietly changed our train and load from the ambulance to the wagon and went on our way rejoicing.

The country having been depopulated under General Ewing's Order No. 11, the men were sorely tried for food, apples being the only edible thing found in Missouri after leaving Lafayette County. The boys would have nearly starved if not for a division of the provisions prepared and taken along for the three men and their wives. From the Grand River our march was without incident until we had reached the Indian Territory. Camping on top of a sharp mountain, we moved at dawn without breakfast. We met seven federals at the foot of the mountain, six of whom we killed. The seventh one took the road south toward Gibson, followed by Captain Gregg, who fired eleven shots, hitting his overcoat nine times. Gregg and his man would shoot awhile and talk awhile. Gregg said, "he never fired at me but I could see the bead on his pistol."

Finally, after Gregg had chased him six miles to higher ground, there were four hundred cavalrymen in plain view, mounted and formed. Of course, Gregg retreated in good order and reported to the command what he had found. George Shepherd, being in command of the men, determined to leave the road. Going east compelled us to recross the Grand River and threw us among the Indians, with whom we were constantly fighting the remainder of the day. The women were kept as far away as practical, though several times they heard the bullets whiz thick and fast. Fortunately, however, they were never frightened. When the fighting had ended, by actual count we had killed forty-five federals, niggers, and Indians with one horse killed as the only casualty on our side. Having crossed the Grand River a third time, we came to an Indian cabin, where they were eating dinner. Hendricks, Gregg, and Mattox entered the house and purloined some meat and bread for their wives. On investigation they found the meat to be dog. The women ate the meat just the same and pronounced it good. Our march from here to Sherman, Texas, was without material interest excepting short rations to the Arkansas River, after which cattle were plenty and we passed sumptuously. Captain and Mrs. Gregg call this trip their bridal tour.[45]

In closing, I desire to say that I have refrained from the mention of names, except of officers, and then only to designate between officers. I have refrained the mention of names among the men because when the fight was on it was utterly impossible to tell who was most meritorious. Any of our veterans would have made good captains.

---

45. Gregg's wife offers her brief recollection of the war, including a recounting of their wedding tour in Gregg, "Can Forgive, but Never Forget," 26–30.

Addendum 1

My War Horse Scroggins

*This particular piece was considered by Gregg himself to be
outside the bounds of his own memoir, but it offers insight into
the wartime experience of Gregg and is worth inclusion here.*[1]

WHEN SHELBY ATTACKED STEEL'S REAR on his (Steel's) march to
Camden in April 1864, I was ordered to take command of our skirmish
line. It was a running fight all day. At sundown in the evening, when
Steel had gone into camp, and Shelby was going into camp in sight of
the enemies' tents, I saw seven Federal infantrymen enter a pine thicket,
which was very dense. I could see only one of my men. I motioned him
to follow me and made a dash for the opposite side of the thicket, the
Federal tents being in fifty yards and men gathering wood for campfires.
I guessed where to enter the thicket to meet the seven infantrymen, met
them, they surrendered to me, I made them lay their arms down and walk
back with their hands up when I dismounted. I passed the seven guns to
my comrade and marched prisoners to Shelby's headquarters. Shelby,
seeing the prisoners, looked about to see who was in charge. When he
saw it was me, he remarked, "Gregg, I will remember you for this day." I
was soon after appointed to the captaincy of Co. "H" Shanks Regiment. I
was ordered on picket that night and accidentally killed my horse with a
stick, so that I had to enter the fight next morning on a superannuated
pony, too feeble to get over a pine log with me on him. However, the fight
did not last long the second day, as Shelby was ordered to repair to Steel's
front and join forces with Price, Fagan, and Marmaduke.

Late that evening after we had camped in close proximity to Steel's
front, I appealed to Major Vivion for a pass to go for a horse, as I was
practically afoot. "I can't do it," says Major Vivion, "but," said he, "you
take Hix and Hi George with you, get horses for them and yourself and

---

1. "My War Horse Scroggins," Quantrill Collection, box 1, folder 30.

I will protect you as best I can." While in winter quarters I had seen an elegant sorrel horse at the place of one Scroggins so that I went directly to his place. On our arrival Scroggins had his wagons loaded and was in the act of starting for Texas. Riding up to Mr. S., I said, "I want the sorrel horse." "Well, sir," said Scroggins, "you can't have him." Said I, "Mr. Scroggins, I am a soldier, you see the animal I ride is unfit for the service. I have this old pony and $1,500 I will give you for the sorrel." "Well, sir, you can't have him," and rode away at once, put a negro woman on the sorrel horse, and started her toward Texas. Scroggins returned, engaged us in conversation, forgetting that we were watching the negro. We bade him a safe journey to Texas. We followed, overtook, and swapped the old pony "even" for the sorrel charger, telling the negro, however, for Mr. Scroggins to come to a farm house not far away, and I would give him the $1,500, but he didn't show up, so it was an even trade. As soon as I had mounted the horse I proclaimed him "Scroggins," and he was ever afterward known by that name. He could trot a mile in three minutes under the saddle.

Soon after the repulse of Steel and Banks, Shelby was ordered to northern Arkansas (White River). In September Shelby was ordered to make a diversion in favor of Price on the Duvall Bluff and Little Rock Railroad. Coming to the railroad a fort loomed up beside the track on the prairie. Shelby halted the command, rode back to our regiment, and ordered us to take that fort on horseback. Lieutenant Colonel Erwin, who was in command of the regiment, was a brave officer but wholly without discretion and with whom I had some differences. Being mounted on Scroggins I was determined that not Erwin nor anyone else should go ahead of me in the fight. After trying for some time to ride the fort down and the horses refusing to go to the breast works, Erwin ordered the men to dismount and take the fort on foot. All this time Scroggins and I had led the attack, twenty feet being as near as I could get to the embankment, and when that close, the enemy would rise and fire at me when Scroggins would drop to the ground on his belly and lay there until the firing ceased, when he would rise up again. Whether this dropping was natural intuition I do not know. I examined him closely for a bullet scalp but could find none. Scroggins never repeated this feat afterwards, and we were in many engagements afterwards. I rode Scroggins through the raid to Missouri, swam him across the Missouri twice. My wife rode Scroggins from Missouri to Texas. On an occasion my wife was telling a friend how the bullets whizzed about her in a fight with the Indians. "Why," said the friend, "weren't you frightened?" "No," she said, "I was on Scroggins and Will was with me."

On my return to the army I left Scroggins with my wife because of his good service and because my wife admired him so much.

Addendum 2

Anderson the Horse Thief

This passage comes from an interview that Connelley did with Gregg on July 14, 1916, years after their falling out. It is unclear what brought them together or what inspired Gregg to speak to Connelley, but the interview generated this brief discussion of Anderson's activities early in the war and Quantrill's reaction to those activities, which may shed light on the disintegration of Quantrill's Raiders almost two years later.[1]

CAPTAIN GREGG TOLD ME THAT IT was early in 1862 that Quantrill first disarmed Bill Anderson and his men. There were but three or four of them. They had been stealing horses from Missourians. Anderson and his men were operating along the Kansas line and near Little Santa Fe. When he disarmed them, Quantrill warned them to not steal anything more where he could get hold of them if they valued their lives.

It seems that Anderson did not heed this warning, for late the following fall he was still stealing. He had some fifteen men, as Gregg remembers. Quantrill was camped on the Blackwater in Johnson County and heard that Anderson and his gang were in that vicinity and had been stealing, and he sent Captain Gregg to bring him in. . . . Meeting them in the road, Gregg rode until his men were opposite and parallel to those of Anderson, then he halted them—halted both columns. He explained his mission and said that he obeyed orders—that for the purpose of those orders and their origin, Anderson and his men would have to look to Quantrill. He demanded that the men hand over their revolvers. Anderson's men complied, saying that Gregg was not to blame. When Anderson and his men were brought before Quantrill, they were sternly dealt with. They were not only disarmed but their horses were taken from them. Quantrill

---

1. William E. Connelley Collection, RH MS 2, box 1, Spencer Research Library, University of Kansas, Lawrence.

told Anderson in short and sharp words that if he ever stole again and he could get hands on him he would hang him and his men to the first tree he came to that would bear their weight. And he sent them afoot and unarmed from camp.

Addendum 3

Gregg Family History

There is no date associated with this brief autobiographical sketch of Gregg's family. It was never intended to be a part of the memoir but seems to offer helpful context for understanding Gregg's origins.[1]

MR. CONNELLEY, I WILL TELL YOU OF MY ANCESTRY, allowing you to write it up in form to suit yourself.

My grandfather Harmon Gregg was born in Kentucky, but at the time of my father's birth, November 1802, resided in Overton County, Tennessee, where he remained until 1807, when he emigrated to Illinois, thence to Missouri in 1812, settled at Cooper's Fort, Howard County, where for several years they were forted against the Indians. Several residents of the fort were killed and scalped by the Indians during their stay. I often heard my father, Jacob Gregg, tell this circumstance to illustrate "old fogyism." Soon after the Indians had been driven back and the settlers dared to leave the fort, a water mill was built on some stream near the fort. Grandfather took a sack of corn to this mill and had it ground. On his return he met a neighbor with corn in one end of his sack and a rock in the other, to balance the corn. Grandfather said to him, "Neighbor, why don't you throw that rock out and divide your corn? It would be lighter on your horse." "O," said the neighbor, "Daddy did this way and he made a good living."

In 1824 my father, Jacob Gregg, made a trip to Santa Fe, Mexico, passing through what is now Jackson County. On returning he persuaded grandfather to move to this territory, settling near where Independence is located, the territory of which Jackson is composed being then under the jurisdiction of Lafayette County court, in which capacity he acted until Jackson County was organized. In November 1826, at the solicitation of Lillian Boggs, afterwards governor of Missouri, Jacob Gregg took the census of the territory composing Jackson County to learn if the

---

1. McClain Library and Archives, University of Southern Mississippi, Hattiesburg.

population was sufficient to organize a county. Mr. Gregg was ten days in taking this census, although he only worked half that time.

Those were days of real hospitality. Coming to a house at or after the turn of forenoon, Mr. Gregg was not permitted to leave until after dinner, besides on entering a house the jug with honey (the people had no sugar) was set out for a toddy. At the taking of this census, Mr. Gregg met with only one rebuff, in Kaw Township, and where he found only seventeen voters, he struck a small settlement of Mormons who never invited him in their houses and were very gruff with him. Mr. Gregg never forgot this rebuff. Think of it, seventeen voters in the township where Kansas City now is. Jackson County was organized in December 1826 on the report of this census, and the county clerk of Jackson County allowed Jacob Gregg ten dollars for taking this census, which is a matter of record in the archives of the county at the county seat, Independence.

When Jackson County was organized, the governor referred the commissioners to locate the county seat to Jacob Gregg as a guide. The commissioners came, hunted up Jacob Gregg, who was living near the present site of Independence, discussed the location of the county seat while sitting on a log where the Independence Court house now stands. Mr. Gregg saw from the trend of their conversation that they were going to locate the county seat on that very spot and remonstrated with them, saying that the law contemplated that the county seat should be located within three miles of the center of the county, and that place was not so near the center. "Well," they said, "it was in three miles of the center of the county proper; it was within three miles of the center of the timbered portion of the county; and the prairie portion would never be settled. O," they said, "there might be an occasional hunter settle on some of the creeks and smaller streams."

Jacob Gregg was first surveyor of Jackson County, second sheriff, serving two terms, was elected representative in the legislature in 1850 on the old-line Whig ticket. Mr. Gregg died in 1893 at the ripe age of ninety-one years, seven months, and two days. Jacob Gregg was married in 1828 to Nancy Lewis, a triplet, one of three girls, all of whom lived to have families. My mother was a native of Kentucky. She lived to be seventy-nine years of age.

My wife's maiden name was Elizabeth E. Hook. Her father, Joseph Hook, was a native of Virginia. He came to Missouri about 1840. Mrs. Gregg's mother was a Carlisle, second cousin to John G. Carlisle. When me and my wife were married, I sent guard to bring a preacher. I did that as a pretense that he was forced to perform the ceremony, that he might not be molested by the federals.[2]

I married my wife about two miles west from Odessa, Missouri. The C&A Railroad runs through the orchard, about one hundred feet from where the house stood. There was about fifty or sixty old comrades present at the marriage, and had the federals come, hell would have been to pay.[3]

2. John Carlisle was a prominent politician from Kentucky. During the war he served in the Kentucky state government. After the war he served as the speaker of the House of Representatives and as the secretary of the treasury for the United States government.

3. The C&A Railroad was the Chicago and Alton Railroad, which ran from east to west across Missouri.

Addendum 4

Documentation of Ownership

*Although the original contract between H. L. Arnold and
Gregg remains elusive, three documents offer a nearly complete
picture of the acquisition and ownership of the memoir.*

CONNELLEY-ARNOLD CONTRACT
FOR RIGHTS TO GREGG MANUSCRIPT

This agreement, made this eighteenth day of January, 1908, by and between William E. Connelley, of Shawnee County, Kansas, party of the first part, and H. L. Arnold, of Jackson County, Missouri, party of the second part, WITNESSETH:

That party of the first part has purchased and hereby purchases from the said party of the second part the manuscript written by Captain William H. Gregg on the border war in which the said Gregg participated and all the letters and papers so written and the benefits of a certain contract between said party of the second part and Captain William H. Gregg, which contract relates to said manuscripts, and which contract is hereby sold and assigned to the party of the first part by the party of the second part.

The party of the first part agrees to pay the party of the second part for the said manuscripts, letters and all papers relating thereto in his possession or to come into his possession, and the benefits of said contract, the sum of one hundred and fifty dollars ($150), said sum to be paid from the first money received by the party of the first part above the expenses of publication from the sale of a book he is now writing on Quantrill and the border wars.

Witness our hands at Topeka, Kansas, the day and your first above written.

(signed) William E. Connelley
(signed) H. L. Arnold

WILLIAM E. CONNELLEY AFFIDAVIT OF
OWNERSHIP OF GREGG MANUSCRIPT
W. C. QUANTRILL
THE MANUSCRIPT WRITTEN BY
CAPTAIN WILLIAM H. GREGG

Harry J. Arnold of Kansas City, Mo., formerly a Special Examiner for the Bureau of Pensions and United States Commissioner, bought this manuscript from William H. Gregg in the spring of 1902, for $90.00. Gregg was not to write another directly or indirectly. Arnold sold this manuscript to me for $125.00, to be paid from first profits from my book. As there never were any profits I suppose he will never get his money. And he has refused to take back the M.S.
Topeka, March 30, 1918.
    William E. Connelley

TITLE PAGE INSCRIPTIONS

These two inscriptions appear on the first and second pages of the copy of the Gregg memoir held by the State Historical Society of Missouri in the University of Missouri's Ellis Library. Apparently the memoir was presented to Connelley in two installments. More importantly, B. J. George Sr. documented Connelley's own handwritten notes on the original Gregg memoir.

Part I
Manuscript once owned by William Elsey Connelley. On the back of Part I the following is written in blue pencil: "The Gregg Manuscript—First Copy—by William H. Gregg.

William E. Connelley."
"This is my copy. WmEE."

B. J. George Sr.
Collections

Part II
Manuscript once owned by William Elsey Connelley. On the back of Part II the following is written in blue pencil: "Second installment of the Manuscript of Captain William H. Gregg.

William E. Connelley"
"My Copy. WmEE."

B. J. George Sr.
Collection

William H. Gregg–
William E. Connelley
Correspondence
(1903–1909)

Kansas City, Mo.
Feby. 11, 1903.

W. E. Connelley, Esq.
My Dr. Sir & Friend.

Yours of yesterday at hand, and also one of much more ancient date. I think my luck has been worse this winter than ever before. First, early in the winter I suffered much inconvenience from a broken rib, then, a day or two after Christmas, when I was boasting of excellent health, I was stricken down with bronchial pneumonia, then it was that I came to the conclusion that my health was not so good. This spell held me indoors for three weeks. Just when I began to think I was well, I had a tooth pulled from which sceptic poisoning set up, and I thought much more about passing my checks than I ever did in battle. I am still confined to the house though my jaw is improving. So you can readily see why I did not answer.

Yes, I saw an account of Sergt. McKenzie's exploits at Baxter.[1] If McKenzie was with Blount, and I suppose he was, his story is a fake, pure and simple. Why, because we had but one man killed in that engagement, Bledsoe, killed by the "band." And, if McKenzie was with the band, he was killed, for I was a witness that the band, driver and all, were killed on the spot.

We had two men killed in the attack on the fort, William Lotspeich and another whose name I have forgotten, but it was neither Rader or Fry.

Further, if either of these men belonged to our Command I did not know them, and if they had belonged, I believe that I would have known them.

---

1. In the text of his book, Connelley offers Sergeant W. L. McKenzie's story of Baxter Springs and how he killed two guerrillas—"Frank Fry and Bill Boder"—and also mentions that the guerrillas intentionally shot a woman and a boy at the fort. He includes Gregg's testimony contradicting McKenzie's story solely in the notes—a great example of how Connelley favored a Union perspective in a guerrilla history. Connelley, *Quantrill and the Border Wars*, 431–32.

Mr. Connelley, the Baxter affair was in Oct. '63, by that period in the war, it has been reputed that Quantrill's men had become as great if not the greatest expert pistol shots in the world, and were rarely caught napping, especially so in time of battle.

Lotspeich and the other man killed at the fort, fell into the hands of the enemy. Bledsoe did not, so that if McKenzie got a pistol from a dead man, he got it from one of the men killed at the fort, neither of whom was named Fry or Rader.

There are big yarns told by both sides that, when run down to facts, many of them at least, prove to be incorrect, if not wholly false.

I have had men tell of some terrible things they did in a certain battle, when I knew positively they weren't there, such men I never mentioned in my memoirs.

Mr. Connelley, I do not think that I could do anything at selling stocks, I am not built that way. My intentions are to move to the country in Mch. or April, I can't do any good in K.C. And, if I can ever get a dollar ahead, I am going to New Mexico and see what I can find digging in the mountains. I have never had much luck at other things, I will try mining. At this time however, I couldn't go down town without walking.

I hope to hear from you soon again.

As Ever Your Friend,

Wm. H. Gregg

———————

K.C. Mo.

May 14, 1903

Friend Connelley.

I called at your office and found the door locked. I met John Noland this morning and made arrangements for him to be at my house at 2 o'clock next Sunday. Can you be there? His story as told to me is a little different from what I expected but of interest just the same.[2]

———————

2. John Noland, referred to here, was a man of much interest to Connelley and subsequent scholars. Noland was a black man who assisted Quantrill and his guerrillas in their war effort. Although there has been much speculation regarding his exact role, ranging from actually wielding a gun and fighting alongside the white guerrillas to merely acting as a body servant, it seems mostly likely that he was used to gather information. Why Noland assisted the proslavery guerrillas is more challenging to understand. It is most likely that Noland, who was mixed race and was likely the son of his owner, had kin among the guerrillas—half-brothers and cousins—and understood the war in the context of these kinship relations and the local power structures of his community.

Hope you will be out, and bring tablet with you as I am running short of writing material.

Yours &c

Gregg.

――――――

At Home, 2103 Forest,
July 31st, 1903.

Friend Connelley.

The next night after you was to see me I came near kicking the "bucket." I was downtown in the evening, had my picture taken, it will be ready tomorrow. I had to hurry home on account of my bowels, called my Doctor, he would not say that I had colera, but, that [I] had every symptom of that disease.

I will send the manuscript with notes by my daughter, Mary. Would be glad to have a word with you before you leave, and have you get picture.

I am too weak to write more.

As ever Your Friend,

Wm. H. Gregg

(PS) I have forgotten your initials, if you cant come out, send name and address.

Gregg.

――――――

2103 Forest Ave.,
Kansas City, Mo.
Sept. 3rd, 1903

My Dear Mr. Connelly,
Chanute, Kansas.

My Dear Sir & Friend.

For a time after you left Kansas City I was very busy doing Carpenter's work, and was too tired to write at night, and now I am laid up for repairs again, rheumatic affection of the side. Am somewhat improved today however.

Well, our reunion has come and gone, nearly fifty responded. John Noland was on hand, wore the badge, seemed to be as proud of it as any of the men.[3]

――――――

3. Noland did indeed attend the Quantrill men's reunions and was something of a celebrity. It seems unlikely that he was accepted in the same way as the other white members

John told me that the reason he failed to show up at 33rd & Troost, was, that just as he got through supper, he was called to drive people he work for. I will try to see him soon and get his story. I will enclose with this the story of my horse "Scroggins." I did not put it in my M.S. because it was not exactly germain to the subject.

I do hope that you will find something for me to do that will be easier than carpentering, beside I am tired of K.C. Rents have gotten to be appalling, and living in proportion, then I am tired of "Catholic" Rule.[4] Let me hear from you soon.

As Ever Your Friend, Wm. H. Gregg.

===========

Kansas City, Mo.
Nov. 24th, 1903

My Dear Mr. Connelly.

After a hard days work, I will try to write you a few lines.

Enclosed you will find clipping from the "Star", giving account of the death of Quantrill's Mother with short (but incorrect) sketch of her. She was born in Pennsylvania, but did not live in Cottage in Springfield, but in Canal Dover. I have been so busy through the week and so tired on Sunday that I have not yet been to see John Noland, think I will appropriate thanksgiving to that task. I have been working at my trade, but it is pretty hard on me. I am getting too old to do that kind of work. I tell you I have to "dig" to make ends meet, living is excessively high here. I do hope that your oil business is proving successful. If I can't be wealthy myself, I would like to see my friends get there just the same.

Mrs. Gregg sends her compliments to you, and joins me in wishing you much success in your new field.

---

of the band, but he appeared to be treated with respect by the other men and was included in the photographs of the band.

4. Gregg is referring to the Irish Catholics who came to power in the Democratic Party in Kansas City during this time. James Pendergast was just beginning to wield his influence during this period to manipulate ethnic voting blocs. His younger brother Tom, known as "Boss Tom," took over in the 1910s and effectively ruled the city until the 1940s. Gregg's ethnic biases appeared to be a greater source of defection from the Democratic Party to the Republican Party than any kind of sectional reconciliation.

I called to see Mr. Arnold two or three weeks since, found him the same jovial, companionable fellow as of yore.[5]

As Ever Your Friend,

Wm. H. Gregg,

2103 Forest Ave.

K.C., Mo.

―――――――――

Kansas City, Mo.

Dec. 8, 1903

Wm. E. Connelly, Esq.

Chanute, Kansas.

My Dear Sir & Friend.

Yours of the 4th inst. at hand, was glad to hear from you.

Yes, I noticed that two by four preachers tirade about the thigh bones, clipped it from the Star to send to you.[6] When I read it, I remarked to my wife that this little pig-head preacher was too narrow to speak to his grand-mother if she had ever passed through a southern state, though the train didn't even stop for water. Your remarks reminded me of a conversation I had with one of Quantrill's men while I was writing my M.S. I told him that I was going to tell the truth allowing the "Chips" to fall where they might. Well, said he, there are some things that ought not to be told, telling of something that Geo. Todd had done. Well, said I, if Geo. Todd did wrong, he should be held accountable or in other words, condemned for those acts, but if he did right, he should have praise for it. Bad deeds committed in the war should be charged to those who committed them. Said I, if these bad deeds are not charged up to those who committed them, then, we who survive will have to rest under the odium, besides, nothing but truth is history, and, if I don't tell the truth as far as I know it, then my work will be condemned, for, said I, the whole truth is going to be told, and it will be told in the near future, and when it is told, it will open the eyes of some people, making some glad and others weep. The South will yet be accorded its proper place in history. Even Quantrill's men will be spoken of more in accord with their just deserts. But we

―――――――――

5. Henry J. Arnold was the man who operated as a go-between for Connelley in acquiring Gregg's memoir.

6. Gregg is likely referring to Two by Twos, a religious movement that began in Ireland and moved to the Americas in the late nineteenth century.

can't get rid of these two by fours, they are being born every day. They are not exactly born 2 by 4's but are taught it by their parents. Now, I would guess that this pig-head preacher McFarland would have a law passed to have every male child born of Southern parents either castrated or put to death. Now you have my opinion of such men as McFarland, no matter what section they are from, or what their politics may be. I have gotten to be a hater of politicians. Why two Republican presidents have admited that under the Constitution the South had a right to secede. Mr. Garfield in his inaugural address, and Mr. Roosvelt in a speech. But you must not tell McFarlan these things for, if you did, he would go back on Roosvelt and damn Garfield's memory forever. I am surprised that McFarlan is not a "Roman Catholic," he ought to belong to that church.

Well I will hush up, I can't do the subject justice.

Well, I went to see John Noland, but the "bird" had flown, he is loving in "Crackers Neck" in his old home neighborhood, but I will catch him of these days.[7]

As Ever Your Friend,

Wm. H. Gregg.

<hr>

Kansas City, Mo.

Nov. 26, /04.

My dear Connelley.

I finally cornered John Noland, sure enough, he was ticklish about telling his story, and when told, it is somewhat different from what I had heard.

John said, I was raised by and belonged to Ausbury Noland, five miles east of Independence. "But", says John, "Befoh you go any further, sah, tell me if this might create any trouble sah." Being assured that it was only for the purpose of perpetuating history, John said, I being a colored man I had the advantage of any white man as a spy. Quantrill had sent a white woman to Lawrence before he sent me, but she failed. It was then the Col. [Quantrill] sent for me to meet him on Little Blue River, and it was there that I received my final instructions, which was to find out the number of soldiers quartered in Lawrence, and if there were any in the near

<hr>

7. Cracker's Neck was not a formal neighborhood but an area in central Jackson County. In a triangle drawn between Independence, Raytown, and Blue Springs, Cracker's Neck was located at the center.

vicinity. The Col. gave me money ample for my expences. I started for Lawrence about the 12th or 14th of August, arriving there I found some colored people there but did not mix with them for fear of recognition. I only spent one day and one night in Lawrence. I counted one hundred and forty soldiers camped about the town but a portion of those left the day I was there. I was not molested while in Lawrence. On my return to Jackson County, I fell in with some of Quantrill's men near Raytown, but told them nothing, for the Col. had told me to tell nothing. Shortly after falling in with these men (who told me the Col. had sent them to escort me to camp) we came in contact with a scout of federals from Independence, we scattered. I saw that I was about to be captured, so I crawled under a schoolhouse and hid my pistols, after a few moments they (the enemy) surrounded the house and I was made a prisoner and taken to Independence where I was held for about ten days, and, notwithstanding the many stories to the contrary, I did not see the Col. or make any report to him until after his return from Lawrence. I was offered $10,000 to betray Quantrill and his men, but refused.[8]

I met John on Election day at Independence, he told me he voted the straight democratic ticket, he said, they tells me that you is a little *off.* Say Connelly, I think that *Hell* broke loose this year, think of it, Missouri went Republican. Well, I was only sorry on account of Cockrell, but I believe it will prove a blessing to him. See what Reesevelt has done, anent that magnaminity, *hurrah for Roosevelt.*

Truly &c

Wm. H. Gregg.

1404 Wabash Ave.,

K.C., Mo.

---

8. Despite no evidence to the contrary, Connelley doubts Noland's story and ultimately refutes it in his history of the war. In a footnote regarding Noland's statement, he said that Noland "seems afraid he might yet have trouble if he should admit that he saw Quantrill after he returned from Lawrence and before the raid. That Quantrill had accurate information of the situation at Lawrence there is no doubt." The implication is clear enough: Noland was lying. See Connelley, *Quantrill and the Border Wars,* 310. Also see Beilein, "'Nothing but Truth Is History': William E. Connelley, William H. Gregg, and the Pillaging of Guerrilla History," in *The Civil War Guerrilla: Unfolding the Black Flag in History, Memory, and Myth,* ed. Joseph M. Beilein Jr. and Matthew Hulbert (Lexington: University of Kentucky Press, 2015), 211–12.

Kansas City, Mo.

Dec. 2, 1904

My Dear Connelly,

Yours of the 28th ult. at hand. Was glad to hear from you. I have been very busy this summer and fall. Through the summer I drove a team at $10 per week, which occupied my entire time, for I will not handle horses and not take care of them, and, when fall came I quit the team and turned my wits, (if I have any) to *politics*, how well I succeeded, you can judge by my returns. However, I made Charley Baldwin a specialty and won by a large majority, (over 4,000,) Now then I am trying to get a place on his staff as deputy sheriff, a place which I believe I filled very satisfactorily under Mr. Pontius, the first *republican* sheriff of Jackson County. I spent three weeks among my old Comrades and friends in the country, a majority of whom pledged me their votes for Charley Baldwin, and, in the majority I think they stood by their pledges, as shown by Washington, a very strong democratic Township, went for Baldwin by 14 votes, and, many of these people voted for Baldwin because I asked them to do so. So, I believe I still have some influence in old Jackson.

As to your inquiry of Quantrill's affair at Morgan Walkers, I think I can tell you the facts in the case, not from participation, for I was not there, but, my old home and the Walker home were only separated about seven miles, and I was intimately acquainted with the Walker family and all the parties participating in the affair, though at this time I can not call to mind the names of all the parties outside the Walker family. I know however that James Bowling, who still lives in Jackson County, was one of the participants. As to the exact date I do not remember. But it was either the latter part of November or early December, 1860. But, before giving you a full rehearsal of the affair, I will try to find out the whereabouts of Andy Walker, son of Morgan, and get the particulars from him. I do not know if I can get the name of the woman Noland spoke of, fact is I have some doubts of the truth of the story.[9]

Yes, some of the boys were arrested and taken to Lawrence, but I only recollect Geo. Mattox who resides at Jeff City, and is a guard at the peni-

---

9. This is not John Noland, as there is no evidence from Connelley or Gregg that he ever spoke directly with the former. Instead, it seems likely to be one of the white Nolands who fought under Quantrill. The woman in question is Morgan Walker's daughter, and the story was that Quantrill orchestrated the raid on the Walker place and flipped sides as merely an attempt to impress her.

tentiary. But I don't think that Geo. went to Lawrence with us, and I think it was so proven at his trial, when he was acquitted.

No, I knew no such man as Joe Bowling, but knew Mark Bowling & Geo. Bowling, both of whom were with Quantrill some, these men are brothers of James Bowling mentioned above. As to the twelve men set apart by Quantrill to do the killing at Lawrence, I know nothing, but believe it to be untrue. As to the story of Cole Younger being opposed to the Lawrence raid, I also believe is untrue. Cole is a man of considerable intelligence, and owing to that fact might have saved his bullets where a man of lesser intellect would not have saved them. As to what Cole did in Lawrence I do not know. I can not call to mind now, that I saw Cole while we were in Lawrence, but do call to mind seeing him often in the fighting on our retreat back to Missouri. I find that both sides are given to exagerations. I believe, yes, I know that as far as I gave details, I gave the correct reasons for our raid on Lawrence, and my recollections that the men were thoroughly agreed on the raid, and, in my estimation, for any man to "wheedle" about it now, is the mereest "rot," be a man, come out on the prairie, "tell the truth" nothing else is history. I ask for place under republicans, and I tell them everything, they know that I was at Lawrence, because I tell them so.

Our friend Arnold gave me a grand letter to Baldwin, for which I am under lasting obligations. Are you personally acquainted with Charley P. Baldwin. It makes no difference. If you are favorable to me, and I believe you are, "fire" a letter at him, at 1308 Locust street, K.C. Mo. without letting him know that I asked it. Any assistance you can give will be appreciated. I could have had a petition a mile long, but preferred special recommendations. The Confederates will meet next Monday night and will endorse me in a body. Let me hear from you soon.

Your Friend As Ever
Wm. H. Gregg.
1404 Wabash Ave.,
K.C., Mo.

―――――――

Kansas City, Mo.
May 13, 1905.

My Dear Connelly.

It has been some months since I wrote you last. Possibly you have thought strange of my silence, but I was only waiting for an event to transpire that I knew would come sooner or later, my appointment to a deputyship in the Sheriff's office. And "I have met the enemy and he is mine." I took office on the 19th of April, and have no fears but I will hold to the end, but I want to assure you that the position is no "snap." I work almost day and night. I have the *itch* 'till my box is clear of paper.

Well, I see that you locked horns with "Rockefeller," and think I can see where you are right, hope you will be successful to the fullest extent.

Well, Connelly, I am going to Louisville, Ky. to the "Johny" reunion, can't you go with me. I am after the Sheriff, Charley Baldwin to go also, he's a prince of good fellows.[10]

I want to thank you for the good letter you sent in my behalf.

Can't you come down to our reunion at Independence on the 22nd August. I mean the reunion of the old guerrilla band. I will insure you a royal welcome. Several of the old boys have passed over the river since our last meeting. It is only a question of a short time when the band will be extinct.

Let me hear from you and tell me how the world is using you.

As Ever, Your Friend,

Wm. H. Gregg,

Sheriff's Office, K.C., Mo.

———————

Kansas City, Mo.

Apl. 30th 1906

My Dear Connelley.

I was so glad to hear from you. I had learned through our friend Arnold that you were in Topeka but he could not give your street number and since I met him which was by accident on a street car. I have not had time to call at his office. I am so busy. The lot of a deputy sheriff is a hard one in this county.

Well, you have found the right man "Randlett" when your letter came I was out on a two days drive through the county, hence, did not get your letter until yesterday, and have been studying about where we were camped when Randlett returned to us, but I have failed to figure out the

———————

10. The reunion referred to by Gregg was the United Confederate Veterans' reunion held on June 14–16, 1905, in Louisville, Kentucky. There would have been tens of thousands of veterans and their families in attendance. It was the last one held in Kentucky. See "United Confederate Veterans Records, 1899–1905," Filson Historical Society, August, 21, 2013, accessed November 30, 2015, http://filsonhistorical.org/research-doc/unitedcon federateveterans/.

place.[11] But it was somewhere in Jackson County Mo. I am sorry that I lost my diary, that would have told many dates and incidents which have slipped my memory. Your version of why Lieut. Randlett tells the story as he does, I think is correct. As to Quantrill's picture, I have a good picture on a button, in fact, all the boys have them. It is the badge we wear at our reunions. I will try to find a photo of this picture and send it to you.

Lieut Randlett is mistakened about his capture, that is, as to who saved him. It was me and not Quantrill, but his version as to why he was saved is correct. There was no one but Todd and I immediately present at the time.

I will relate an incident that occurred at the time of Lieut Randlett's capture that he also may remember. Immediately after Randlett's capture a man drove up in a two horse wagon. The near one a "chestnut" sorrel mare, white stripe in face. I got this mare and rode her while Lieut Randlett was with us. I want you to tell Lieut Randlett that I am proud to know that he still lives and that I send him an invitation to attend our next reunion, and will see to it that he has a cordial welcome. I will also see that a written invitation is sent to him. I will write up the McIntosh incident as soon as I get moved and straightened up at 2629 Holmes Street. Accept my best wishes.

As Ever Your Friend.

Wm. H. Gregg

Kansas City, Mo.
May 13th 1906

My Dear Conelley.

In my first reply to yours of April 25th there were many questions I did not answer. I have no recollection of the man "Ellis" but there was some promiscuous shooting. It was a cold morning in Feby 1862. Randlett's version of the skirmish near Asbury is correct. As to the deserters, or thieves, I do not remember the particular circumstance, as there were other similar circumstances. I do not recall Randlett's Independence experience, it may not have been brought to my notice before. I do not know of a "lock" of Quantrill's hair taken from his head while in Missouri, but saw the bunch that Scott procured from the grave, which

---

11. Reuben Randlett claimed to be the Union officer who Quantrill sought to exchange for Perry Hoy. The story of Randlett's capture appeared in Connelley, *Quantrill and the Border Wars*, 225–34.

was about the same shade as I remember it. I thought however, that the hairs Scott exhibited was a little more of a sandy caste than Quantrill's hair, but, being so long underground may have caused the difference, or changed the color. I recollect the man "Potter" but can recall nothing of his history. But as to Quantrill's arrest at Bonham Texas, I know only by information from others, Quantrill was placed under arrest by Brig. Gen. McCullough. And, as I have heard it, Quantrill unbuckled his belt as if to hand his arms to McCullough. When his men gathered around him and demanded that he not give up his arms, when he immediately unbuckled his belt and left McCullough's office. McCullough immediately ordered his militia under arms [and] sent them in pursuit of Quantrill, in which pursuit Anderson and his men and some of Quantrill's former followers joined, and, that a trivial skirmish ensued before Quantrill had crossed the Red River, when he had crossed Red River, he was out of Mc-Cullough's jurisdiction and the pursuit ended. I do not know the exact cause of Quantrill's arrest, possibly Potter's version is right. In my little sketch I aimed to avoid writing of things that I was not personally cognizant. In fact I intended it should be more a biography of myself.

As I am somewhat under the weather, I will defer the McIntosh incident until another time.

As Ever Your Friend.

Wm. H. Gregg

2629 Holmes St.

K.C. Mo

———

K.C. Mo.

July 6th 1906

My Dear Connelley

Yours of 4th just at hand. Yes Josiah Gregg was uncle to me, he was born in Tenn. about the date you mention. And my Grand Father's name was Harmon. Came to Mo. in 1812, settled in Cooper's Fort in Howard County, where the sons + daughters grew up to man + womanhood. Came to Jackson County in 1825, settled about four miles N.E. of Independence where he remained until the sons and daughters were married except Josiah, who was never married. I think I told you of the circumstances of Uncle Josiah building the clock for the priest in Santa Fe. If you have Uncle's book, "Commerce of the Prairies" you will see a picture of a man leading, or trying to lead a mule, underneath of which are the words, "damn a mule anyhow." Samuel Gregg is an older brother of mine who lives near Independence. As to the amount of land, and the price paid for it, I am not able to say, nor do I know for what amount it was sold. The land was sold to a Mr. Anderson I think and is still in the hands of the Anderson family. Recollect I am speaking of Grand Father's land or homestead. I am of the opinion that uncle Josiah never worked any land in Jackson County, although he may have. I would suggest that if you want to get the real facts in the matters in hand, that you come down and spend about a week with me, when I will take great pleasure in showing you around and assisting you in any way I can.[12]

We will have our reunion on the 30th August at Independence may be you had better be there.

As Ever

Wm. H. Gregg

Kansas City, Mo.
Oct. 2nd 1906

My Dear Mr. Connelley.

By accident I obtained an item that I had long since given up as lost. The death of my favorite Brother brought about this communication. The death of Brother having been published in the Kansas City Star, although the notice in the Star was intended more as a slur than in remembrance, fell into the hands of John C. Van Gundy of Neosho Rapids Kas. whom I knew when we were boys, and who was a witness to the dastardly acts of Jim Lane's marauders on the Neosho River in Sept. 1856 and whose sister, Mrs. Chris Carver was murdered by them. Mr. Van Gundy sent me his reminiscences of the early settlers and early times and tragedies of those days.

Van Gundy informs me that Capt. John E. Cook afterwards hanged with John Brown was the leader of this band. In this party, were several men who lived in the immediate vicinity. I wish you would come down before I return Van Gundy's reminiscences. My thought are so engrossed with my work in the sheriff's office that I really have no time to write these notes as they should be written.

------

12. Josiah Gregg was most well known for his two-volume book, *Commerce of the Prairies* (1844), a travel book that described what became the southwestern part of the United States in the early 1840s.

Well, Connelley, I think we will make a clean sweep of "Shannonism" this fall, and if we do I am going to invite you to dinner.
Let me know hear from you.
>   As Ever Your Friend.
>   Wm. H. Gregg
>   1215 Wabash ave
>   Kansas City, Mo.

———————

>   Kansas City, Mo.
>   Feby 26th 1907

My Dear Mr. Connelley,

I received your prospectus for Doniphan's Expedition today. I think well of your understanding, fact is I am much interested in your book, so much so that I will in the near future send you the subscription price for the book.

Since the reception of your prospectus, I have wondered if you got the incident of the clock in your book. My friends have been clamoring at me about my little book. I have had inquiries from California, from a library in St. Louis, and many other places, besides my many friends in this and adjoining counties. And even Kansans have sent requests for the book when it is published. It is time that all these old animosities, sentimental-ities, [et cetera] should be cast to the four winds. We are all Americans and that is why the fight was so hard, and last so long. I believe that the most vicious article I have seen was from the pen of a democrat ex. Gov. T.T. Crittenden, a man whose war record is almost, if not altogether as unsavory as that of the Kansas Red Leg. I used to in my younger days, answer the articles of these unsavory gentry, but of late years, I have re-frained. About all that old Tom Crittenden has is blood money derived from the assassination of Jesse James.[13]

I am still with the Sheriff, and think that I will remain to the end of his present term.
>   Your Friend As Ever
>   Wm. H. Gregg
>   1307 Michigan Ave
>   K.C., Mo.

———————

13. Thomas Crittenden infamously facilitated the killing of Jesse James by the Ford brothers. See Stiles, *Jesse James*, 376–80. As this comment about the former governor makes quite clear, Gregg did not renounce his loyalties to his guerrilla brethren or to the South-ern community when he became a Republican.

Kansas City, Mo.
May 19th 1909

W.E. Connelley Esq.
Topeka Kansas
My Dear Sir + Friend,

Yours of 17th inst at hand. Am sorry to say that I can't go to Topeka next Saturday. As I am expecting to be appointing to a position by the board of police commissioners. But, after my appointment will write you when I can go.

Very Truly +c
Wm. H. Gregg
K.C. Mo
1707 E. 37th St.

816 Lincoln Street
Topeka, Kansas, June 30, 1909.

Captain William H. Gregg:
Kansas City, Mo.,
Dear Captain:

I thank you for your kind favor of the 28th instant. I had formed the opinion that Wayman could not be relied on, but did not doubt that he was a good soldier. I have no doubt that he killed William E. Hopper, as he says. He became very angry at me when I told him that Quantrill could not have been born in Maryland, and that there was no truth in the story that he and his brother had been set on by Jayhawkers and his brother killed, etc.

I think the memory of Morgan T. Mattox quite good, and he impressed me as truthful and sincere. He thinks a good deal of you and said he would like very much to see you and Mrs. Gregg. But he is extremely bitter towards Cole Younger, and says the other comrades are the same, but would not tell me why. The only thing in which I find him mistaken is his story that he and Jesse James rode side by side in the charge at Centralia. In checking up that statement I found that Jesse was not at Centralia at all, but was lying wounded near home in Clay or Ray county. I find the book written by Jesse James Jr., to be wholly unreliable. I am not much impressed with the soldierly qualities of either Frank or Jesse James. Frank James told Walter Williams that he was at the battle of Wilson Creek, which I know is wholly untrue. When Frank is over in Kansas he always tells that he was sick and not with Quantrill at Lawrence, but I know he was at Lawrence. His denying it in Kansas is wholly unnecessary, for there is no feeling in Kansas on the matter and has not been for many years. He would be just as safe in Lawrence as in his mother's house in Clay County.

In writing my Life of Quantrill I found an article written by Mrs. Sara T. L. Robinson, widow of Governor Charles Robinson, who lived at Lawrence at the time of the raid, in which she says she heard Captain Gregg say "Wheel left and kill every man, woman and child". In my book I say that Captain Gregg never gave such an order in his life, and that he would have shot any man heard giving such an order. I also say that the honor of no woman was violated at Lawrence, and I enumerate instances where many guerrillas interposed and saved lives. I have the statement of a Mr. Grovenor that Bill Anderson saved his life. I also set out the indignities shown the dead body of Skaggs. I have tried to state just the facts. I do not, of course, believe the raid was justifiable, and think it murderous and outrageous, and not called for by any rule of civil war. And many of the guerrillas were needlessly brutal and murderous, but instances of kindness and manliness must be credited to even them if they did any. I have many letter written by Quantrill.[14]

I wish you could come up and spend a day or two with me. I want to publish your manuscript before long, and I should like to go over it carefully with you before printing it. Some places ought to be fuller, and there are a few places where it ought to be changed a little.

Your friend truly,

Kansas City, Mo.
June 28th 1909

My Dear Mr. Connelley,

Yours of 19th inst at hand would say in reply that Morg Mattox was with Quantrill. Went South in company with my wife [and] I. He was

---

14. The letter to the editor by Sara Robinson that Connelley refers to does not state that "Captain Gregg" gave an order to kill women and children. It clearly states that a bushwhacker by the name of Captain Grear made the above statement. There is no mention of any Gregg. Perhaps Connelley supposed that Robinson meant to say Gregg, but she most certainly did not. It does seem that he is using this as a contrived opportunity to tell Gregg just how much he has gone out of his way to stand up for him. If there was a bushwhacker named Grear, he does not appear on any lists. One must wonder how Robinson would have known any of the bushwhackers' names, especially during such a chaotic scene. See Sara Robinson, "Gov. Robinson in the Raid," *Topeka Daily Capital,* October 12, 1908.

only a boy about 15 but joined after I left the company. Yes George Todd was killed near, and about ¼ mile west from Staples farm. I can't give you section [et cetera] but can get in at reunion in August. Todd fell in with Shelby about Waverly or Lexington and did scout duty for the army until killed. Todd left Shelby at the crossing of Little Blue, and was killed where he reentered Independence [and] Lexington road, he halted his men a short distance from the road telling them it was dangerous for them to go to the road, [and] he went to road to reconnoiter, and was killed at long range, something like ¼ mile. Staples farm is about 2½ miles NE from Independence. Personally I do not know what point Quantrill started from to Kentucky, however, my understanding is that he started from the "Austin" farm 3 miles south from Lexington. I know nothing of a Wiggington farm near Waverly, but think the Wiggington family lived somewhere in Lafayette Co. after order #11. I am sure that Hudspeth is wrong, I know nothing of the Kimmel farm, but there was a "Kinsey" farm 10 miles E, of Independence. Bone Hill was simply a country church, situated almost directly East from Independence about 16 miles. Hambright Hill is on Independence [and] Lexington road about 2½ mile E. from Sibley and about the same distance NE from Buckner.[15]

I am not sufficiently posted to give you names of men who went to Ky with Quantrill but know you have some names wrong, for instance you have Billy Gall, should be "Gaw." I have no recollection of an Ed or Bill Noland but Henry Noland was with us. I have no recollection of a Bill Robinson. I don't think Cy Flannery went to Ky. Chard Renic should be "Chat" Renic. Geo. Shepherd didn't go to Ky with Quantrill but did command the party with whom my wife and I went South.

My understanding is that Quantrill took 41 or 42 men to Ky. I don't know who left Quantrill at the Miss. River other than Koger [and] the Hudspeth's, I know of no Dupees (Dupey's) in Lafayette Co. there were Dupey's in Jackson, near Pleasant Hill, they may have gone to Lafayette under order #11.

I do not know who killed Maj. Curtis. I was with Jarrett [and] Younger in the chase of 17 men (don't know what state they were from) in a

---

15. George Wigginton (spelled incorrectly in the census as "Wigington"), who fought under Quantrill during the war, lived in Jackson County before the war. The Wiggintons were a part of the Fristoe clan—a larger kinship network spread through Jackson County and beyond. 1860 Federal Manuscript Census, Jackson County, Mo. Nonetheless, they almost certainly migrated to Lafayette County or even further east after Order 11. There were Fristoes in Lafayette and Chariton Counties and Wiggintons in Boone County. 1860 Federal Manuscript Census.

northwesterly direction, and killed one of the party myself about 140 yds. I can't say if any more were killed, I stopped when I killed the man. Wayman is full of gas, but, was a good soldier. Now, the old hard shell Baptist Eight Cornered log church, long since gone, we had not yet captured Randlett.

We were at the church on the 20th March, Quantrill was surrounded in Tate House on night of 22nd and Randlett was captured afterwards. Randlett may have been told of Halleck's order, and Quantrill may have joked him in the way Wayman says, but, I don't recollect.

You are correct as to Jesse James, he never was with Quantrill, nor was he at Centralia, he might have entered the service as early as the latter part of June 1864, he was sometimes with Todd [and] sometimes with Anderson so I am told, he went south in company with me + wife '64.

The farm of Capt. Perdee (not Pardee) is located on Blackwater Creek about 4 miles west of south from Columbus, and about 5 or 6 miles S.E. of Chapel Hill, and 8 or 10 miles east from Lone Jack.

We started south the 1st of October (or about that time) 1863, not '64 as you wrote, from the farm of Capt Perdee camping 1st night on Grand River Cass Co. second night, beyond the Osage River, we saw no enemy till Baxter. I will give names of our party on our Bridal Tour as far as I can recollect, Geo Shepherd, Jesse James, Jas Johnson [and] Pin Indian, Johnson's Bro, Jas A. Hendricks, Dick Mattox, Morgan Mattox, (no kin to Dick) Joe Hall, Matt Wayman, Harrison Trow, ____ Ranaberger, Henry Terry, Andrew M. Clay, Long Stevens, and myself, is as far as I can now remember, then the three women, my wife, Mrs. Jas A. Hendricks, my sister, and Mrs. Dick Mattox.

I believe I have answered all your questions as far as I know,

As Ever

Wm. H. Gregg

1707 E 37th St.

---

816 Lincoln Street
Topeka, Kansas, August 13, 1909

Captain William H. Gregg,
Kansas City, Mo.,
My dear Captain:

Please write me when and where your re-union is to be held this year. I went to see Mr. Randlett yesterday and asked him to go with me and he said he would if he could get off from the job he has, which is remodeling a house. He has to have it done by a certain day, and it may be that he can not get off. He will come if he can. I also invited Hon. Cyrus Leland, Jr., to go with me, and he said he would if he could get away from the duties of his office. Leland commanded the immediate forces that contended with you in the retreat from Lawrence and says he would like to talk with you.[16]

Yours truly,

[signature missing]

―――――――

Kansas City, Mo.

Aug 14th 09

Wm. E. Connelley Esq

Topeka Kansas

My Dear Mr. Connelley

Yours of 13th inst at hand. Our reunion will be held at Independence on the 20th and 21st days of this month. We are governed by Friday and Saturday nearest the 20th day of August. We adapted this method on account of the weather conditions.

I do hope that you will bring both Leland and Randlett and I now very cordially invite them to be present and will insure to them and to you a cordial welcome. Jackson County is experiencing as hot weather as I ever felt in my 71 years here.

Regards to self and family,

As Ever Your Friend.

Wm. H. Gregg

K.C. Mo

1707 E. 37th St.

―――――――

16. Born in Wisconsin in 1841, Cyrus Leland had moved with his family to Kansas as a part of the migration of abolitionists to the territory in an effort to stop the spread of slavery. He was a young lieutenant on Thomas Ewing's staff during the summer of 1863. Based on some of the notes in his book, it was evident that Leland served as an informant for Connelley. At different points he consulted Leland and even allowed him to read some of his source material, such as Gregg's memoir. See Connelley, *Quantrill and the Border Wars*, 165, 199, 302, 405. For Leland's account of the skirmishing after the Lawrence raid, see ibid., 397–419.

816 Lincoln Street,

Topeka, Kansas, August 26, 1909

Captain William H. Gregg,

Kansas City, Mo.,

My dear Captain:

I enclose you a carbon copy of the letter I am sending to Governor Hadly to-day for you. I hope you will get this place. I know that if you get it you will hold it as long as you live if you want to.

I want you move every think you can to get the place. See all the men I suggested, and see every other man of influence that you can. I believe you can get the place.

If there is anything else I can do please let me know and I will do it at once and do it gladly.

If it is not too awfully hot I will go to Higginsville to meet the veterans of the Mexican War, and will do what I can there, if I find anything I can do.

Your friend truly,

[signature missing]

———————

Kansas City, Mo.

Aug. 31st 1909

My Dear Mr. Connelley,

I write to thank you for the sentiments expressed of my wife and myself in your letter Gov. Hadley. I had a splendid interview with the Governor yesterday. He was not aware of the perfidy of John B. Stone, until told by my friend Mr. Heitman, who has voluntarily taken up my cause, and the good women of the daughters of the Confederacy have also voluntarily taken up my cause, a committee of whom had a conference with Mr. Hadley at Swope Park yesterday afternoon. And I now think, that my chances are far better than they ever were before.[17]

Allow me again to offer the thanks of Mrs. Gregg and myself for those splendid sentiments.

I am as ever Your Friend.

Wm. H. Gregg

———————

17. Herbert Hadley was a Kansan by birth but later moved to Saint Louis. Before being elected governor of Missouri in 1908, he was the attorney general of the state and successfully broke the Standard Oil Trust there. He was no doubt an acquaintance of Connelley, as Connelley had tried to take on Standard Oil earlier in the decade.

Bibliography

Primary Materials

UNPUBLISHED MATERIALS

Denver Public Library, Denver, Colo.

William Elsey Connelley Papers.

Ellis Library and State Historical Society of Missouri, Columbia

George, B. James (1896–1975), Collection, 1887–1975, (c3564).
Gregg, William H., "A Little Dab of History Without Embellishment," [1906], (c1113).
Union Provost Marshals' File of Papers Relating to Individual Citizens. Microfilm, Special Collections.
United States Federal Manuscript Agricultural Census.
United States Federal Manuscript Census.
United States Federal Manuscript Census Slave Schedules.

McCain Library and Archives,
University of Southern Mississippi, Hattiesburg

William C. Quantrill Collection.

Spencer Research Library, University of Kansas, Lawrence

William E. Connelley Collection.

PERIODICALS

Confederate Veteran, 1907
Frank Leslie's Illustrated Newspaper, 1863, 1865
Harper's Weekly, 1863
Kansas City Times, 1910
Topeka Daily Capital, 1908

PUBLISHED MEMOIRS AND EARLY HISTORIES

Agriculture of the United States in 1860, Compiled from the Original Returns of the Eighth Census by Joseph C. G. Kennedy, Superintendent of the Census. Washington, D.C.: Government Printing Office, 1864.

Bailey, Joseph. *Confederate Guerrilla: The Civil War Memoir of Joseph M. Bailey*. Edited by T. Lindsay Baker. Fayetteville: University of Arkansas Press, 2007.

Burch, John P. *Charles W. Quantrell: A True History of His Guerrilla Warfare on the Missouri and Kansas Border during the Civil War of 1861 to 1865*. As told by Harrison Trow. Vega: J. P. Burch, 1923.

Connelley, William Elsey. *Quantrill and the Border Wars*. Cedar Rapids: Torch Press, 1910.

———. *James Henry Lane: The "Grim Chieftain" of Kansas*. Topeka: Crane, 1899.

———. *John Brown*. Topeka: Crane, 1900.

———. *Wyandot Folk-Lore*. Topeka: Crane, 1899.

Cummings, James. *Jim Cummins, The Guerrilla*. Excelsior Springs: Daily Journal, 1908.

Dalton, Kit. *Under the Black Flag*. Memphis: L. J. Tobert, 1995.

Eakin, Joanne Chiles, ed. *Recollections of Quantrill's Guerrillas: As Told by A. J. Walker of Weatherford, Texas to Victor E. Martin in 1910*. Independence, Mo.: Two Trails, 1996.

Edwards, John N. *Noted Guerrillas, or the Warfare of the Border*. Saint Louis: H.W. Brand, 1879.

Fitch, Edward, and Sarah Fitch. *Postmarked: Bleeding Kansas, Letters from the Birthplace of the Civil War, Pioneer Dispatches from Edward and Sarah Fitch*. Edited by Chad Lawhorn. Purple Duck Press, 2013.

Gregg, Josiah. *Commerce of the Prairies*. 1844.

Hildebrand, Samuel. *Autobiography Of Samuel S. Hildebrand*. Edited by Kirby Ross. Fayetteville: University of Arkansas Press, 2005.

McCorkle, John. *Three Years with Quantrill: A True Story*. Written by O. S. Barton. Notes by Albert Castel. Commentary by Herman Hattaway. Norman: University of Oklahoma Press, 1992.

Statistics of the United States in 1860; Compiled from the Original Returns and Being the Final Exhibit of the Eighth Census. Washington, D.C.: Government Printing Office, 1866.

United Daughters of the Confederacy, Missouri Division, comp. *Reminiscences of the Women of Missouri during the Sixties*. Dayton: Morningside Press, 1988.

U.S. War Department. *The War of the Rebellion: A Compilation of the Official Records of the Union and Confederate Armies*. 128 vols. Washington, D.C.: Government Printing Office, 1880–1902.

Watts, Hamp B. *The Babe of the Company: An Unfolded Leaf from the Forest of Never-to-be-Forgotten Years*. Fayette: Democrat-Leader Press, 1913.

Younger, Thomas Coleman. *The Story of Cole Young, by Himself*. Chicago: The Henneberry Company, 1903.

———. *Confessions of a Missouri Guerrilla: The Autobiography of Cole Younger*. Reprint, Saint Paul: Minnesota Historical Society Press, 2000.

Secondary Materials

PRINT

Bailey, Anne, and Daniel E. Sutherland, eds. *Civil War Arkansas: Beyond Battles and Leaders.* Fayetteville: University of Arkansas Press, 2000.

Beilein, Joseph M., Jr. *Bushwhackers: Guerrilla Warfare, Manhood, and the Household in Civil War Missouri.* Kent: Kent State University Press, 2016.

———. "The Guerrilla Shirt: A Labor of Love and the Style of Rebellion in Civil War Missouri." *Civil War History* 58, no. 2 (June 2012): 151–79.

Beilein, Joseph M., Jr., and Matthew Hulbert, eds. *The Civil War Guerrilla: Unfolding the Black Flag in History, Memory, and Myth.* Lexington: University of Kentucky Press, 2015.

Benedict, Bryce D. *Jayhawkers: The Civil War Brigade of James Henry Lane.* Norman: University of Oklahoma Press, 2009.

Berry, Stephen W. *All That Makes a Man: Love and Ambition in the Civil War South.* New York: Oxford University Press, 2003.

———, ed. *Weirding the War: Stories from the Civil War's Ragged Edges.* Athens: University of Georgia Press, 2011.

Blight, David W. *Race and Reunion: The Civil War in American Memory.* Cambridge: Harvard University Press, 2001.

Bowen, Don R. "Counterrevolutionary Guerrilla War: Missouri, 1861–1865." *Conflict* 8 (1988): 69–78.

———. "Guerrilla War in Western Missouri, 1862–1865: Historical Extensions of the Relative Deprivation Hypothesis." *Comparative Studies in Society and History* 19 (January 1977): 30–51.

———. "Quantrill, James, Younger, et al.: Leadership in a Guerrilla Movement, Missouri, 1861–1865." *Military Affairs* 41 (February 1977): 42–48.

Brownlee, Richard S. *Gray Ghosts of the Confederacy: Guerrilla Warfare in the West, 1861–1865.* Baton Rouge: Louisiana State University Press, 1958.

Castel, Albert E. *Civil War Kansas: Reaping the Whirlwind.* Lawrence: University Press of Kansas, 1997.

———. "Quantrill's Bushwhackers: A Case Study in Partisan Warfare." *Civil War History* 13 (March 1967): 40–50.

———. *William Clarke Quantrill: His Life and Times.* New York: F. Fell, 1962.

———. *William Clarke Quantrill: His Life and Times.* Norman: University of Oklahoma Press, 1999.

Castel, Albert E., and Thomas Goodrich. *Bloody Bill Anderson: The Short, Savage Life of a Civil War Guerrilla.* Lawrence: University Press of Kansas, 1998.

Clinton, Catherine, and Nina Silder, eds. *Divided Houses: Gender and the Civil War.* New York: Oxford University Press, 1992.

Earle, Jonathan H., and Diane Mutti Burke. *Bleeding Kansas, Bleeding Missouri: The Long Civil War on the Border.* Lawrence: University Press of Kansas, 2013.

Etcheson, Nicole. *Bleeding Kansas: Contested Liberty in the Civil War Era.* Lawrence: University Press of Kansas, 2004.

Fellman, Michael. *Inside War: The Guerrilla Conflict in Missouri during the American Civil War.* Oxford: Oxford University Press, 1990.

Foote, Lorien. *The Gentlemen and the Roughs: Violence, Honor, and Manhood in the Union Army.* New York: New York University Press, 2010.

Fox-Genovese, Elizabeth. *Within the Plantation Household: Black and White Women of the Old South.* Chapel Hill: University of North Carolina Press, 1988.

Franklin, John Hope. *The Militant South, 1800–1861.* Urbana: University of Illinois Press, 1956.

Gallagher, Gary W. *The Confederate War.* Cambridge: Harvard University Press, 1997.

Gallagher, Gary W., and Kathryn Shively Meier. "Coming to Terms with Civil War Military History." *Journal of the Civil War Era* 4 (December 2014): 487–508.

Geiger, Mark W. *Financial Fraud and Guerrilla Violence in Missouri's Civil War, 1861–1865.* New Haven: Yale University Press, 2010.

Gerteis, Louis S. *The Civil War in Missouri: A Military History.* Columbia: University of Missouri Press, 2012.

———. *Civil War St. Louis.* Lawrence: University Press of Kansas, 2001.

Goodrich, Thomas. *Black Flag: Guerrilla Warfare on the Western Border, 1861–1865.* Bloomington: Indiana University Press, 1999.

Greenberg, Amy S. *Manifest Manhood and the Antebellum American Empire.* New York: Cambridge University Press, 2005.

Harris, Charles F. "Catalyst for Terror: The Collapse of the Women's Prison in Kansas City." *Missouri Historical Review,* 83/3 (April 1995): 290–306.

Hoffer, Peter Charles. *Past Imperfect: Facts, Fictions, Fraud—American History from Bancroft and Parkman to Ambrose, Bellesiles, Ellis, and Goodwin.* New York: Public Affairs, 2004.

Hulbert, Matthew C. "Constructing Guerrilla Memory: John Newman Edwards and Missouri's Irregular Lost Cause." *Journal of the Civil War Era* 2, no. 1 (March 2012): 58–81.

———. *The Ghosts of Guerrilla Memory: How Civil War Bushwhackers Became Gunslingers in the American West.* Athens: University of Georgia Press, 2016.

———. "Guerrilla Memory: Irregular Recollections from the Civil War Borderlands." PhD diss., University of Georgia, 2015.

Janney, Caroline E. *Remembering the Civil War: Reunion and Limits of Reconciliation.* Chapel Hill: University of North Carolina Press, 2013.

Linderman, Gerald F. *Embattled Courage: The Experience of Combat in the American Civil War.* New York: Free Press, 1987.

Mackey, Robert R. *The Uncivil War: Irregular Warfare in the Upper South, 1861–1865.* Norman: University of Oklahoma Press, 2004.

McKnight, Brian D. *Confederate Outlaw: Champ Ferguson and the Civil War in Appalachia*. Baton Rouge: Louisiana State University Press, 2011.

———. *Contested Borderland: The Civil War in Appalachian Kentucky and Virginia*. Lexington: University Press of Kentucky, 2006.

McPherson, James M. *The War That Forged a Nation: Why the Civil War Still Matters*. New York: Oxford University Press, 2015.

Miller, Brian C. *John Bell Hood and the Fight for Civil War Memory*. Knoxville: University of Tennessee Press, 2010.

Mountcastle, Clay. *Punitive War: Confederate Guerrillas and Union Reprisals*. Lawrence: University Press of Kansas, 2009.

Mutti Burke, Diane. *On Slavery's Border: Missouri's Small-Slaveholding Households, 1815–1865*. Athens: University of Georgia Press, 2010.

Myers, Barton A. *Executing Daniel Bright: Race, Loyalty, and Guerrilla Violence in a Coastal Carolina Community, 1861–1865*. Baton Rouge: Louisiana State University Press, 2009.

Myers, Barton A., and Brian D. McKnight, eds. *The Guerrilla Hunters: Irregular Conflicts during the Civil War*. Baton Rouge: Louisiana State University Press, 2017.

Neely, Jeremy. *The Border between Them: Violence and Reconciliation on the Kansas Missouri Line*. Columbia: University of Missouri Press, 2007.

Noe, Kenneth W. "Who Were the Bushwhackers? Age, Class, Kin, and Western Virginia's Confederate Guerrillas, 1861–1862." *Civil War History* 49 (2003): 5–26.

Noe, Kenneth W., and Shannon H. Wilson, eds. *The Civil War in Appalachia: Collected Essays*. Knoxville: University of Tennessee Press, 1997.

Novick, Peter. *That Noble Dream: The "Objectivity Question" and the American Historical Profession*. Cambridge: Cambridge University Press, 1988.

Oertel, Kristen Tegtmeier. *Bleeding Borders: Race, Gender, and Violence in Pre-Civil War Kansas*. Baton Rouge: Louisiana State University Press, 2009.

O'Flaherty, Daniel. *General Jo Shelby: Undefeated Rebel*. Chapel Hill: University of North Carolina Press, 2000.

Piston, William G., and Richard W. Hatcher III. *Wilson's Creek: Second Battle of the Civil War and the Men Who Fought It*. Chapel Hill: University of North Carolina Press, 2000.

Ponce, Pearl T. *Kansas's War: The Civil War in Documents*. Athens: Ohio University Press, 2011.

Schultz, Duane. *Quantrill's War: The Life and Times of William Clarke Quantrill, 1837–1865*. New York: St. Martin's Press, 1996.

Silber, Nina. *Gender and the Sectional Conflict*. Chapel Hill: University of North Carolina Press, 2008.

———. *The Romance of Reunion: Northerners and the South 1865–1900*. Chapel Hill: University of North Carolina Press, 1993.

Smith, W. Wayne. "An Experiment in Counterinsurgency: The Assessment of Confederate Sympathizers in Missouri." *Journal of Southern History* 35 (August 1969): 361–80.

Stiles, T.J. *Jesse James: Last Rebel of the Civil War.* New York: Vintage, 2003.

Sutherland, Daniel E. *American Civil War Guerrillas: Changing the Rules of Warfare.* New York: Praeger, 2013.

———. *A Savage Conflict: The Decisive Role of Guerrillas in the American Civil War.* Chapel Hill: University of North Carolina Press, 2009.

———. "Sideshow No Longer: A Historiographical Review of the Guerrilla War." *Civil War History* 46 (March 2000): 5–23.

Whites, LeeAnn. *The Civil War as a Crisis in Gender: Augusta, Georgia, 1860–1890.* Athens: University of Georgia Press, 1995.

———. *Gender Matters: Civil War, Reconstruction, and the Making of the New South.* New York: Palgrave Macmillan, 2005.

———. "Forty Shirts and a Wagonload of Wheat: Women, the Domestic Supply Line, and the Civil War on the Western Border." *Journal of the Civil War Era* 1 (March 2011): 56–78.

Whites, LeeAnn, and Alecia P. Long, eds. *Occupied Women: Gender, Military Occupation, and the American Civil War.* Baton Rouge: Louisiana State University Press, 2009.

Witt, John Fabian. *Lincoln's Code: The Laws of War in American History.* New York: Free Press, 2013.

Wood, Kirsten E. *Masterful Women: Slaveholding Widows from the American Revolution through the Civil War.* Chapel Hill: University of North Carolina Press, 2004.

Wyatt-Brown, Bertram. *Southern Honor: Ethics and Behavior in the Old South.* New York: Oxford University Press, 1982.

WEBSITES

Ancestry.com. ancestry.com.

Filson Historical Society. "United Confederate Veterans' Records, 1899–1905." August 21, 2013. http://filsonhistorical.org/research-doc/united confederateveterans/.

Missouri Secretary of State website. http://www.sos.mo.gov/.

The Lawrence Massacre by a Band of Missouri Ruffians under Quantrell. Lawrence, Kans.: J. S. Broughton, 1863. Available at Kansas Collection. June 30, 1994. http://www.kancoll.org/books/cordley_massacre/quantrel.raid.html.

The War of the Rebellion: Official Records of the Civil War. Washington, D.C.: Government Printing Office, 1880–1901. Available at Ohio State University Ehistory. http://ehistory.osu.edu/osu/sources/records/.

Index

Italic numbers represent pages where art appears.

African Americans, 21, 23, 25, 36, 47, 69, 81
Anderson, William T. "Bloody Bill," 25, 32, 33, 62, 77; at Baxter Springs, 74–75; horse thief, 83–84, 104, 108, 110; at Lawrence, 15, 70; usurpation of Quantrill, 17–18, 26, 34, 76
Arnold, Harry J., 6, 7, 88, 89, 97, 101, 102

Baldwin, Charley, 100, 101, 102, 106
Banks, Nathaniel, 81
Barker, John, 77
Barnhill, John, 77
Bassham, William, 77
Battles. *See name of specific battle*
Baxter Springs, Battle of, *16*, 17, 26, 33, 74–76, 93
Big Creek, Mo., 53, 60
Bledsoe, William, 70, 72, 75, 93, 94
Blue Cut, Mo., 53
Blunt, Andrew, 32, 50–51, 52, 62
Blunt, Gen. James G., 74–76
Boggs, Lillian, 85
Bone Hill, Mo., 58, 109
Bowling, George, 101
Bowling, James, 100
Bowling, Mark, 101
Brown, John, 33, 105
Brownlee, Richard S., 9–10, 37–38
Buel, James T., 56
Burch, Col. Jim, 63–64
Burnt District, 17
Burris, James, 67
Burris, Col. John T., 58, 66

Canal Dover, Ohio, 29, 36, 47, 48, 96
Cane Hill, Battle of, 61
Carthage, Mo., 61, 74
Carver, Mrs. Chris, 105

Castel, Albert, 38–39, 41–42
Centralia, Battle of, 18, 76, 107, 110
Chiles, Dick, 59
Chiles, Kit, 56
Clark, Kate, 27
Clark, Samuel, 51
Clay, Andrew M., 110
Clement, Archie, 33
Cockrell, Jeremiah Vardaman, 56
Columbus, Mo., 58
Confederate army, 20, 26, 34, 74
Confederate Home, Higginsville, Mo., 7
Connelley, William Elsey, 2, 5, 19, 20, 27, 32, 43, 83, 85; correspondence with Gregg, 93–112; ownership of Gregg memoir, 88–90; *Quantrill and the Border Wars*, 8–10, 37–38; relationship with Gregg, 4–10; shaping guerrilla history, 37–41
Cook, John E., 105
Copland, Lt., 57
Cowherd, Henry, 64
Crawford, Jeptha, 66–67
Crawford, Mrs. Jeptha, 41, 66–67
Crittenden, Thomas, 106
Crump, Mrs. Samuel, 47
Cummings settlement, 67
Curtis, Maj., 75

District of the Border, *13*, 14, 15
Doniphan's Expedition, 106
Doors, Jerre, 55

Edwards, John N., 38–39, 42; *Noted Guerrillas*, 5, 35–36
Eldridge Hotel, 70
Emancipation Proclamation, 33
Erwin, William H., 81
Estes, Daniel or Alvis, 51
Ewing, Thomas, 14, 15, 72–73, 78

Fagan, James F., 80
Federals. *See* Union soldiers
Fellman, Michael, 39–42
Fort Blair, 17, 33
Fort Leavenworth, 57
Fort Smith, 61
Foster, Maj., 56
Fry, Frank, 93

Gamble, Hamilton Rowan, 63
Garfield, James A., 98
Garrison, Mrs., 59
Gaugh, Billy, 77
General Order 11, 15, 17, 78
George, B. J., 19, 90
George, Hi, 80
George, Hicks, 53, 80
Germans (Union soldiers), 51
Gilchrist, Joe, 50
Gill, Marcus, 30
Glasscock, Dick, 77
Gleaves, Harvey, 58
Glenn, Frank, 19
Graham, Jack, 77
Gregg, Harmon (grandfather), 85, 104
Gregg, Jacob (father), 21, 51, 85–86
Gregg, Josiah (uncle), 104
Gregg, Lizzie (née Hook; wife), 26, 77–79,
    81–82, 86–87, 97, 108–10, 112
Gregg, Samuel (brother), 105
Gregg, William H., 3; ambush of Sessions,
    23–24, 62–63; assault of *Sam Gaty*, 23,
    62; at Baxter Springs, 17, 74–76; central-
    ity of guerrilla war to Civil War, 19–20; as
    Charley Hart, 48; correspondence with
    Connelly, 93–112; on Lawrence raid,
    65–75; motivations for writing memoir,
    1–4, 48; omissions of memoir, 2, 23–24;
    on Quantrill, 47–48; relationship with
    Connelley, 4–10; understanding of his-
    tory, 1, 7, 47, 48, 97
Guest, Hiram, 77

Hadley, Herbert, 112
Hall, Joe, 110
Halleck, Henry, 12, 22, 49, 58, 110
Haller (Hallar), William, 56, 60
Hampton, John, 54
Hannibal, Mo., 52
Harrison, Capt., 60
Hart, Charley. *See* Quantrill, William Clarke

Hart, Joe, 63–64
Hartville, Battle of, 61
Hayes, Upton, 53, 56–57
Heitman, 112
Hendricks, James A., 20, 47, 64, 77–79,
    110
Herndon, Dr., 51
Higbee, Charley, 73
Hook, Lizzie. *See* Gregg, Lizzie
Hopper, William E., 107
Horton, J. C., 69–70
Houk, Bob, 53
Hoy, Perry, 22, 50, 56–58
Hudspeth, 109
Hughes, J. T., 56
Hulbert, Matthew C., 35

Independence, Mo., 15, 23, 47, 49, 51,
    53; battle of, 56, 59, 66–67, 76, 85–86,
    98–99, 102–5, 109, 111
Indian Territory, 30, 61, 78

Jackson, John, 64
Jackson, Thomas "Stonewall," 1, 35
James, Frank, 77, 107
James, Jesse, 18, 106, 107, 110
Jarrette, John, 76
jayhawkers, 10, 12, 15, 20, 24, 28, 29, 30,
    47, 107
Jennison, Charles, R., 66
Johnson, A. V. E., 76
Johnson, James, 110

Kansas City *Star*, 49, 96, 97, 105
Kentucky, 9, 18, 34, 77, 85, 86, 109
Keshlear, John, 51
Koger, John, 20, 47, 51–52, 109

Lane, James, 66, 105
Lawrence raid, 10, 15, 17, 20, 108, 111;
    Gregg's account, 24–25, 65–74, 100–
    101; John Noland's account of 98–99;
    Quantrill's role in 32–33
Lee, Robert E., 1, 35
Leland, Cyrus, 111
Lewis, Warner, 61
Lexington, Mo., 18, 58, 76, 109
Little, James, 62, 64, 77
Little, John, 30
Lone Jack, Mo., 56, 67
Long, Peyton, 77

Longacres, 57
Lost Cause (narrative), 1, 35–36, 41
Lotspeich, William, 93–94
Lowe house fight, 50–51

Marmaduke, John S., 61, 80
Mattox, Dick, 77–79, 110
Mattox, George, 54, 100
Mattox, Morgan T., 107, 108, 110
McCorkle, John, 36
McCulloch, Henry E. (McCullough), 104
McFarland (preacher), 98
McKenzie, W. L., 93–94
Missouri *Republican*, 57
Montgomery, James, 47–48
Moore, Ezra, 55
Morris, Henry, 65

Nash, Lt., 50
Noland, Asbury (or Ausbury), 98
Noland, Henry, 109
Noland, John, 95–96, 98–99, 100
Noted Guerrillas (Edwards), 5, 35–36

O'Donnell, Pat, 59
Official Records of the War of the Rebellion, 31
Olathe, Kans., 57–58

Penick, Bill, 59, 62, 66
Perdee, Capt., 67, 74, 110
Perry, Joab, 71–72
Pike's Peak, 47
Pink Hill, 51–52
Platte City, Mo., 52
Plattsburg, Mo., 63–64
Pleasant Hill, 15, 53, 58, 109
Pontius, Mr., 100
Pool, Dave, 17, 32, 54–55, 62, 74, 76
Port, Dr., 51
Potter, 104
Prairie Grove, Battle of, 61
Price, Sterling, 26, 34, 75–77, 80–81
Provost Marshals' Files Relating to Individual Citizens, 40

Quantrill, Caroline Cornelia Clark (mother), 29, 36, 47–48, 96
Quantrill, William Clarke, 28, 43, 83; as architect of guerrilla war, 27–34; in Gregg-Connelley correspondence, 88, 89, 94, 96–101, 103–4, 107–10; in

Gregg memoir, 47–62, 65, 67–77; as guerrilla, 10–18; origin story, 27, 47–48; as subject of history, 34–42
Quantrill and the Border Wars (Connelley), 8–10, 37–38

Ranaberger, 110
Randlett, Reuben, 102–3, 110, 111
Renick, Chat, 77, 109
Robinson, Charles, 108
Robinson, Sara T. L., 108
Roosevelt, Theodore, 98, 99

Saint Joseph, Mo., 52
Saint Louis *Globe Democrat*, 73
Sam Gaty (boat), 23, 25, 62
Samuels residence, 65
Santa Fe Trail, 59, 68
Saunders, Col. Jim, 66–67
Saunders, Mrs. Jim, 66–67
Scott, Ferdinand, 58, 61–64
Scott, W. W., 36, 48, 103, 104
Scroggins (Gregg's horse), 80–82, 96
Scroggins, Mr., 81
Searaucy, 53, 60
Sessions, Capt., 23–24, 62–63, 64
Shanks, David, 80
Shawnee Town, Kans., 59–60
Shelby, Joseph Orville "Jo," 61, 76, 80–81, 109
Shepherd, George, 78, 109, 110
Sherman, William Tecumseh, 49
Sibley, Mo., 59, 62, 65, 69, 109
Simmons, 58
Skaggs, Larkin, 69–70, 108
Slavery, 2, 21, 31, 33, 36
Smiths Fork, Platte River, 64
Smithville, 64
Soper, Mr. 63
Southern Historical Society, 35
Springfield, Battle of, 61
State Historical Society of Missouri, 19, 43, 90
Steel, Larkin, 69
Steele, Frederick, 80
Stevens, Long, 110
Stone, John B., 112
Stony Point, 51

Tate house fight, 23, 50, 57, 110
Taylor, Fletch, 64

Terry, Henry, 110
Texas, 17, 26, 30, 34, 36, 74, 76, 77, 78,
    81, 104
Todd, George, 25, 32, 52, 53, 59, 60, 61,
    62, 77, 97, 103, 110; at Baxter Springs,
    74–76; death of 109; at Lawrence, 68,
    71, 73; usurpation of Quantrill, 18, 26,
    33–34, 76
Trow, Harrison, 36, 110
Tucker, James, 51
Tucker, William, 54

Union soldiers, 25, 30, 51, 54–56, 58, 64,
    68, 74, 78, 80, 87, 99; attacks on south-
    ern households, 14–15, 17, 66–67,
    72–73; employing counterinsurgency
    measures, 12–15, 22–23, 49; pursuit of
    guerrillas after Lawrence, 70, 72

Van Gundy, John C., 105
Vidette, 67
Vivion, H. J., 80

Walker, Andrew, 10, 12, 27, 28, 30, 36, 37,
    100
Walker, Morgan, 28, 29, 30, 36, 100
Washington, George, 49
Wayman, Matthew?, 107, 109–10
Wellington, Mo., 58
Westport, Mo., 58
Wigginton family, 109
Williams, Walter, 107
Wilson's Creek, Battle of, 21
Woodsmall, 57

Younger, Cole, 32, 56, 62, 74, 76, 101, 107,
    109
Younger, James, 77

New Perspectives on the Civil War Era

*Practical Strangers: The Courtship Correspondence of Nathaniel Dawson
and Elodie Todd, Sister of Mary Todd Lincoln*
EDITED BY STEPHEN BERRY AND ANGELA ESCO ELDER

*The Greatest Trials I Ever Had:
The Civil War Letters of Margaret and Thomas Cahill*
EDITED BY RYAN W. KEATING

*Prison Pens: Gender, Memory, and Imprisonment in the
Writings of Mollie Scollay and Wash Nelson, 1863–1866*
EDITED BY TIMOTHY J. WILLIAMS AND EVAN A. KUTZLER

*William Gregg's Civil War: The Battle to Shape
the History of Guerrilla Warfare*
EDITED AND ANNOTATED BY JOSEPH M. BEILEIN JR.

Printed in the United States
By Bookmasters